AUTOMATE
YOUR
GROWTH

A 12-Minute Daily Habit, Build Authenticity, Remove Resistance, Unlock Unstoppable Success

By

PRADEEPKUMAR K PADMANABHAN

DEDICATED TO

My Parents & Teachers

WHY IS THIS BOOK FOR YOU?

Unlike conventional self-help books that focus on motivation and willpower, Automate Your Growth provides a practical, structured system that makes personal transformation effortless. The key is alignment, not struggle.

- No more overthinking - Success becomes automatic.

- No more inconsistency - Small, daily actions lead to massive transformation.

- No more burnout - You grow without force, stress, or resistance.

This book is for anyone who wants to:

- Break free from self-doubt, procrastination, and overthinking

- Develop a daily practice that guarantees growth

- Align personal and professional success effortlessly

- Achieve prosperity, freedom, and purpose - without struggle

Your Journey Starts Now!

Commit to just 12 minutes a day, and watch how effortlessly your life transforms. Are you ready to automate your growth and unlock the unstoppable version of YOU?

ACKNOWLEDGMENT

With deep gratitude and reverence, I express my heartfelt appreciation to all those who have been a guiding light on my journey, leading to the creation of this book.

I bow in gratitude to my beloved parents, M. Padmanabhan Nair and K. Devaky Nessiar—even though they are not physically present, their blessings, values, and unconditional love continue to guide and inspire me every moment. Their presence is felt in every step I take, and this book is a tribute to the foundation they built for me.

I extend my deepest reverence to my spiritual Gurus:

Sri Sri Ravi Shankar, Sri Ramakrishna Paramahamsa, Ramana Maharshi, Osho Rajneesh, Adi Shankaracharya, J. Krishnamurti, and many other enlightened souls—who have illuminated my path with their wisdom and teachings.

A special note of appreciation to my New Age trainers and coaches—T. Harv Eker, Surendran Jayasekar, Siddharth Rajsekar, Thaddeus Lawrence, Blair Singer, Rajiv Talreja, Puja Puneet, Prachi Mayekar, Robert Riopel, Aaron M. Huey, and many more—who have shaped my perspective on personal growth, success, and transformation.

I hold immense admiration for my role model, Dr. APJ Abdul Kalam, whose life and vision continue to inspire me.

To my wife, Cinderella, my unwavering pillar of support, and to my children, Adhree and Niyatee, for their love, patience, and encouragement—I am forever grateful. My brother, sister, uncles, family members, and dear friends have stood by me, making this journey meaningful.

I also acknowledge Som Bathla and Ravi Lalit Tewari, who have been invaluable coaches and guides in my journey as an author.

Every person I have met, every challenge I have faced, and every book I have read has contributed to my learning and growth. These experiences, combined with the wisdom of countless mentors, have led to the birth of this book.

I must acknowledge the pivotal role of Technology and AI tools like ChatGPT in shaping this book and accelerating its publication. These innovations have been invaluable thinking partners, refining my ideas, enhancing my expression, and making the journey of bringing this book to life both efficient and enriching.

Above all, I express my deepest gratitude to the universal power that signalled my intellect to embark on this journey. Without this predesigned guidance, this book would not have been possible.

I extend my sincere thanks to the publishers of this book for bringing my work to the world and to my students, whose curiosity, dedication, and pursuit of growth continue to inspire me every day.

This book is a humble offering to all seekers of growth, success, and authenticity. May it serve as a guiding light in your journey of transformation. Jai Hind!

PREFACE

My friend, have you ever felt like life is an endless checklist? Every situation demands something new—a skill to master, a behavior to refine, an expectation to meet. I know that feeling well.

As a child, my mother gave me simple advice: "Smile at everyone you meet on your way to school." It sounded easy, but I turned it into a task—something I had to remember to do rather than something that came naturally.

School was no different. "Study for this many hours," the teachers said. I did. I memorized, followed the rules, and still felt exhausted. Later, when I had to speak in public, I faced another long list of instructions—stand tall, modulate your voice, use hand gestures, maintain eye contact. Again, I was more focused on ticking off steps than actually communicating.

Life felt like a constant act of remembering how to behave instead of simply being myself.

I started to wonder: What if there was a way to grow without constantly forcing it? What if I didn't have to think so hard about smiling, studying, or speaking—what if it all just happened naturally?

That's when I realized something profound: The more authentic we become, the more effortless life feels.

When we stop trying to be what others expect and simply align with who we truly are, something shifts. Resistance fades. Growth stops feeling like a struggle. We start responding to life—not out of pressure or fear—but with ease, clarity, confidence and joy.

This book is about that shift.

****

The 12-Minute Habit That Changes Everything

I wanted to find a way to make growth effortless—to create a practice that would eliminate unnecessary struggle and allow personal transformation to happen automatically.

That's how I discovered a simple yet powerful 12-minute daily habit—a habit that rewires the mind, strengthens values, and brings clarity without overwhelming effort.

This habit isn't about adding another task to your day. It's about removing resistance, simplifying your growth, and unlocking the natural flow of life.

Imagine:

- Preparing for challenges effortlessly, without overthinking.

- Speaking and acting with confidence, without forcing it.

- Meeting people and connecting authentically, without self-doubt.

- Growing in every area of life—health, wealth, relationships, career, and beyond—without feeling overwhelmed.

This habit isn't just about success—it's about becoming the best version of yourself naturally.

****

Why This Book Matters

For over 30 years, I have worked across government, public, and private sectors, as an entrepreneur, coach, and mentor. I've helped engineers and professionals break free from limitations and design lives of happiness, freedom, and financial success.

But my approach isn't about quick fixes or motivational hype. It's about creating a structured, repeatable, and deeply authentic path to growth.

This book is not another self-help theory—it's a practical system that you can apply immediately. Each chapter builds on the last, guiding you through:

- Automate – Learn how to make growth effortless by aligning with natural success patterns.

- Habit – Implement a simple, 12-minute daily habit to rewire your mind for continuous progress.

- Authentic – Discover who you truly are and remove the resistance that holds you back.

- Values – Establish a strong foundation with six core values that shape your decisions and actions.

- Growth – Expand in all areas of life—health, wealth, relationships, career, and beyond.

- Money – Master money secrets and use wealth as a tool for freedom and fulfillment.

- Unstoppable – Step into a state of flow where growth happens automatically, without struggle.

The goal? To make personal growth as automatic as breathing.

****

Your Journey Starts Now

So, my friend, if you're tired of chasing success, if you're done with overthinking, self-doubt, and resistance, this book is for you.

Give yourself just 12 minutes a day—that's all it takes. I promise you, the results will be life-changing.

Let's take this journey together. Let's unlock effortless growth, limitless potential, and unstoppable success.

Are you ready? Let's begin.

Don't just believe—take action and see the results. This habit isn't about believing without doing; it's about taking steps and experiencing the change.

May this habit bring you authenticity, abundance, and happiness in your life. Let me know how it works for you—I'd love to hear your experiences!

Feel free to reach out for any clarifications and share your thoughts.

You can contact me at: pradeepdesign@gmail.com

For Your Growth & Happiness

Pradeepkumar K Padmanabhan

www.pradeepkumarkp.com

★ ★ ★

Table Of Contents

INTRODUCTION

Hello my friend,

Have you ever felt stuck—like no matter how much effort you put in, you're not seeing the growth you want? You set goals, push yourself, try new strategies, but something always slows you down. The struggle feels endless.

But what if I told you that growth doesn't have to be a struggle? That success, happiness, and financial freedom can be automatic—not something you chase, but something that naturally unfolds?

That's exactly what this book is about.

I'm here to show you a proven, structured process that aligns your mind, habits, values, and actions—so that you don't have to keep forcing growth. Instead, you'll move into a state of effortless success.

Why Growth Feels Hard (And Why It Doesn't Have to Be)?

Most people struggle with growth because they resist life's natural flow. They overthink, doubt themselves, and repeat the same cycles, making progress feel slow and painful. But here's the truth:

- The universe already runs on automation. The sun rises, rivers flow, and seasons change—without stress.

- Your body is designed for automation. Your heart beats, your breath flows, and your mind processes thoughts—without you forcing them.

- Success works the same way. If you build the right system, growth happens naturally—just like it was always meant to.

The problem? Most people fight against this natural rhythm. But when you remove resistance and follow a structured path, you tap into a flow where growth becomes inevitable.

This book is that structured path.

The Path to Automating Your Growth

To truly automate growth, we need to follow a logical sequence—one that builds on itself and transforms every part of your life.

Here's how this book will guide you through that journey:

Chapter 1: Automate – Why struggle when you can grow naturally?

The biggest myth about success is that it requires constant effort. But the truth is, life itself operates on autopilot—planets orbit, trees grow, and nature evolves without force. This chapter will show you how to align with the natural rhythm of success so that you no longer feel like you're pushing a rock uphill.

- Why struggle is unnecessary for growth.

- How to sync your actions with the flow of success.

- The mindset shift that makes growth automatic.

Chapter 2: Habit – A 12-minute daily system that transforms everything.

Success isn't about doing more—it's about doing the right things consistently. This chapter introduces a simple but powerful daily habit that rewires your brain for success.

- A 12-minute practice that makes progress inevitable.

- Why willpower and motivation are not the key to success— habits are.

- How small, daily actions lead to massive, long-term change.

Chapter 3: Authentic – Growth isn't about changing—it's about becoming more of who you already are.

Most people struggle because they try to force themselves into a version of success that doesn't align with who they really are. In this chapter, you'll discover how to strip away external conditioning and reconnect with your true self.

- How to remove self-doubt and fear of judgment.

- Why being authentic makes success effortless.

- How to stop chasing a life that doesn't truly fulfill you.

Chapter 4: Values – Your values shape your success, whether you realize it or not.

Without strong values, success is fragile. This chapter helps you identify and strengthen the six core values that make success sustainable:

- Courage – The ability to act despite fear.

- Clarity – Knowing exactly what you want.

- Consistency – The habit of taking action daily.

- Capacity – Expanding your ability to handle challenges.

- Consciousness – Staying fully aware and intentional.

- Caring – Success that benefits others, not just you.

When these values become part of who you are, you stop second-guessing yourself and start making decisions with confidence.

Chapter 5: Growth – Success isn't just about money—it's about growth in all areas.

Many people succeed in one area of life while neglecting others. Real success is holistic. This chapter helps you expand in:

- Health – Energy and well-being fuel success.

- Wealth – Financial stability gives you freedom.

- Relationships – Meaningful connections create happiness.

- Career – Your work should be fulfilling, not draining.

- Recreation – Fun and relaxation are essential.

- Spirituality – Inner peace leads to clarity and direction.

- Contribution – Helping others brings deeper fulfillment.

If you've ever felt imbalanced—this chapter will help you realign and grow in all areas simultaneously.

Chapter 6: Money – Money is not the only goal—freedom is.

Money isn't just for paying bills—it's a tool to create freedom, impact, and security. This chapter helps you shift your mindset around money and teaches you how to:

- Earn money by creating real value.

- Manage money smartly and without stress.

- Use money to fund your growth, experiences, and contributions.

When you stop seeing money as a struggle and start using it as a tool, financial success becomes effortless.

Chapter 7: Unstoppable – The final step: entering the flow state of success.

This is where everything comes together. Once you remove resistance, build strong habits, and align with your values, success stops being something you chase—it becomes something that naturally flows to you.

- Live without fear or hesitation—fully trusting your path.

- Experience success as an effortless process—no more burnout.

- Step into your highest potential—where opportunities come to you, rather than you chasing them.

At this stage, growth is no longer something you force—it's something that happens automatically.

What This Book Will Do for You

- No more overthinking – You'll finally break free from doubt and hesitation.

- Consistency without struggle – Growth will feel natural, not forced.

- True transformation – You'll stop "trying" and start living in flow.

- Freedom in every sense – Financial, emotional, and spiritual freedom.

- Living with purpose & impact – Each day will have meaning and clarity.

How to Get the Most Out of This Book

- Commit to the process – Growth isn't a one-time event; it's a way of life.

- Start your 12-minute habit – This one practice will change everything.

- Trust the flow – Stop forcing things. Align with who you are meant to be.

- Apply what you learn – The only way to grow is to take action.

This is Just the Beginning

Everything you need for success is already inside you. The universe is guiding you. Now, take the first step:

- Dedicate 12 minutes a day.

- Embrace your core values.

- Trust the process.

- Step into the life you were meant to live!

The framework of Automate Your Growth

The framework of this book follows a logical, step-by-step transformation where each element builds upon the previous one, leading to prosperity, freedom, and purpose. Here's how they are linked:

The 12-Minute Process (Daily Habit)

- A structured, repeatable practice that helps you to reflect, refine, and reinforce your True Self.

- This habit of discovering your authentic personality, automate your growth without feeling life overloaded with tasks.

Enables Authenticity (Discovering Your True Self)

- The 12-minute habit helps individuals identify and align with their true values, strengths, and purpose.

- By becoming self-aware, they make better decisions and reduce external dependency for validation.

Develops The 6 Core Values (Courage, Clarity, Consistency, Capacity, Consciousness, Caring)

Authenticity naturally leads to the development of these six essential qualities:

- Courage – To embrace change and challenges.

- Clarity – To set meaningful goals and direction.

- Consistency – To stay committed to growth.

- Capacity – To build new skills and expand potential.

- Consciousness – To make mindful, purpose-driven choices.

- Caring – To create positive impact in relationships and society.

Strengthens Personal & Professional Growth

When these six values become part of your daily life:

- Personal Growth: In 7 areas of personal growth: health, relationships, wealth, career, recreation, contribution and spirituality, more time we spend in our career growth.

- Balanced Life: Growth in all areas without burnout.

- Professional Growth: Career growth, whether its job/or business results to high income that supplement other areas progress

Yes, career growth—whether through a job or business—leads to high income, which in turn fuels progress in other areas of life. Here's how this linkage works in your framework:

****

Career Growth as the Driver of High Income

- Advancing in a job (promotions, leadership roles, skill mastery) or

- Scaling a business (entrepreneurial success, innovation, and market positioning) Results in

- High Income – Increased financial stability, wealth creation, and opportunities.

****

High Income Fuels Growth in Other Areas

- Wealth → Financial Freedom (Investments, security, abundance)

- Health → Better access to medical care, nutrition, and wellness programs

- Relationships → More quality time, better experiences with loved ones

- Recreation → Freedom to travel, explore hobbies, and reduce stress

- Contribution → Ability to give back, support causes, and mentor others

- Spirituality → Peace of mind and focus on deeper purpose

****

Leads to Prosperity, Freedom & Purpose

- Prosperity – Achieving financial and emotional abundance.

- Freedom – Breaking free from external pressures, creating a self-driven life.

- Purpose – Living a meaningful, impactful life aligned with one's true self.

The Growth Cycle Continues

- The 12 Minute Daily Habit to to reflect, refine, and reinforce your True Self.

- Through this habit, you are discovering your authentic personality, cultivating core values, and fostering holistic growth.

- As financial stability increases, personal and professional growth accelerate.

- More resources → More learning, better networks, and higher growth potential.

- This leads to prosperity, freedom, and purpose—sustainable success!

Thus, **Unlock Unstoppable Success**

- The 12-minute habit → builds authenticity

- Authenticity → strengthens the 6 core values

- The 6 values → drive personal growth

- Personal growth → ensure professional growth

- Growth → leads to prosperity, freedom, and purpose

This automated growth cycle ensures long-term success and fulfillment.

Chapter 1

Automate

1. The Universe is on Autopilot—So is Life

You've seen how the world is obsessed with automation, right? Everything—from smart homes to self-driving cars—is designed to make life easier, faster, and more efficient. AI is handling tasks with zero hesitation. No second-guessing. No distractions. Just seamless execution.

Now, here's a thought—if machines can automate processes so effortlessly, why can't we do the same for our own lives?

Think about it. Why do we struggle with overthinking, inconsistency, and resistance? Why do we sabotage our own progress when we know exactly what would make our lives better?

Imagine if your thoughts, decisions, and actions naturally aligned with growth—without effort. No more internal battles. No more procrastination. Just pure, unstoppable momentum.

Sounds like a fantasy? It's not. It's actually how the universe already works.

Look at the Universe- It's Already Running on Autopilot

Take a step back and observe. The sun rises and sets, the seasons change, planets move in perfect harmony—all without hesitation. Do they ever "not feel like it" one day? Do they overthink their next move?

No. Because they follow a natural order—a rhythm that never wavers.

Now, compare that to how we operate. We hesitate. We overanalyze. We create unnecessary struggles in our minds—fears, doubts, and stories about why we're not ready.

But here's the truth: Reality doesn't wait for us. It moves with or without our permission. What seems overwhelming today could shift in an instant. So why waste energy resisting the flow?

The Secret to Automating Your Growth

You don't need to force growth. You just need to remove the resistance.

Decide Once – The universe doesn't hesitate, and neither should you. Make growth non-negotiable. No more "should I or shouldn't I?"—just act.

Set Systems, Not Just Goals – AI works because it follows a program. So should you. Design daily habits that run on their own, so progress happens naturally. The less you rely on willpower, the easier it gets.

Trust the Process – When you stop resisting and start flowing with life, everything feels lighter. Growth stops being a battle and starts becoming second nature.

At the end of the day, automation isn't just about machines—it's about you. The goal isn't to struggle through growth. It's to make growth your default setting.

And here's where it gets really interesting...

If life is on autopilot, where does free will come in? Are we just following a script, or do we have the power to rewrite it?

Let's explore that next: Life's Grand Design—The Balance of Free Will and Destiny.

2. Life's Grand Design: The Balance of Free Will and Destiny

My friend, let's pause for a moment and talk about something that might just shift the way you see life.

Have you ever wondered—how much of your life is truly in your control? Are you actually making choices, or are you just following a script that was written long before you were even aware of it?

The answer is both simple and profound: Life is already designed, yet you are free.

Sounds like a contradiction, right? But let's break it down.

1. Life is Already Designed—It Moves on Its Own

Look around. The sun rises and sets, the seasons change, and your heart beats without you even thinking about it. Rivers flow effortlessly toward the ocean, stars continue their cosmic dance, and nature unfolds in perfect rhythm.

Now, what if I told you that your life also follows a design? That every challenge, every opportunity, and even the people who cross your path are all part of an intricate, pre-set pattern?

But here's where it gets interesting—you are not a prisoner of this design. You have a role to play. And that role is shaped by your free will.

2. Free Will and Destiny: Two Partners in the Dance of Life

Think of destiny as a river. It has a direction—it's always moving toward something. Now, picture yourself as a boat on this river.

- You cannot change the direction of the river—that's your destiny.

- But you can decide how you row, how fast you move, and whether you fight the current or flow with it—that's your free will.

This is how life works: Destiny provides the path, but free will determines the experience.

Now, let's break it down even further:

- Fate is what you are given—your circumstances, challenges, talents, and opportunities.

- Destiny is your highest possibility, the purpose your life is moving toward.

- Free Will is your power to choose—how you respond, what actions you take, and how you shape your own journey.

3. The Only Place You Can Act: The Present Moment

Here's the truth: The past is untouchable. The future is unpredictable. The only place where free will exists is now.

So, what can you do with this moment?

1. Accept Where You Are – Fighting reality only drains your energy. Accept your fate, and then decide how you want to respond.

2. Define Where You Want to Go – Clarity of purpose aligns you with your destiny. Who do you want to become? What impact do you want to make?

3. Make Conscious Choices – Every action, no matter how small, shapes your future. Be intentional.

4. Trust the Flow of Life – Some things are beyond your control. Instead of resisting, adapt, learn, and keep moving forward.

4. Life Feels Effortless When You Align with Your Purpose

When you stop fighting the flow and align your free will with your destiny, life stops feeling like a struggle.

Here's how you can live in harmony with your life's design:

- Cultivate Self-Awareness – Understand what truly matters to you.

- Balance Action with Surrender – Take bold steps, but also trust that the universe is guiding you.

- Be Grateful – Gratitude helps you see perfection in every moment.

- Focus on Contribution – The more you give, the more life gives back.

5. The Magic of Realizing This Truth

Most people live at one of two extremes:

- They either think they control everything and burn themselves out trying to force life into submission.

- Or they believe they have no control and drift aimlessly, waiting for fate to decide their future.

But when you understand the balance between free will and destiny, everything changes.

- Challenges stop feeling like obstacles and start looking like stepping stones.

- Failures stop feeling like punishments and start becoming powerful lessons.

- Success stops being just about effort—it becomes about alignment.

And most importantly... you are never alone.

Life itself is communicating with you—through intuition, through synchronicities, through moments of deep realization. The more you tune in, the clearer everything becomes.

Trust the Dance of Life

My friend, life isn't a battle to be won. It's a dance to be enjoyed.

Some steps are yours to take. Some rhythms are set by the universe. But when you learn to move with grace—to balance free will and destiny—life unfolds effortlessly.

So, trust the process. Keep rowing your boat. And let the river take you exactly where you're meant to be.

Now, if free will plays such a powerful role, how can we use it to automate our growth and make success feel natural?

Let's explore that next: The Foundation of Automated Growth.

3. The Foundation of Automated Growth

You know, most people believe that growth is hard—that they have to struggle, push, and force themselves to improve. But what if I told you that real growth happens effortlessly when the right conditions are set?

Think about it. Does a tree struggle to grow? Does a river force itself to flow? No. Growth is natural when you align with the way life actually works. You don't have to fight your way to success; you just need to step into the flow.

Let me share something with you that might change the way you grow—forever.

1. Keep Thoughts to a Bare Minimum

Have you ever noticed that the more you think, the harder things feel?

Your mind can either be your greatest tool or your biggest trap. When it's filled with unnecessary chatter, it slows you down—like driving a car with the handbrake on. Overthinking is resistance. The key is to keep only the thoughts that serve you and let go of the rest.

Want to make growth automatic?

Think less. Do more. - Lesser Thoughts, Better Life!

2. Mission to Action—No Space for Doubt

Between your mission and your action, there should be nothing—no hesitation, no second-guessing, no unnecessary emotions.

Think of it like jumping into a cold pool. If you stand there debating how cold it'll be, you'll never jump. But if you just dive in, the water adjusts to you instantly.

Growth works the same way—just act, and everything else will align.

3. Emotion is Also an Action That Creates Results

Most people think emotions are just feelings, but they're much more than that. Every emotion is an action waiting to happen.

- Anger makes you react.

- Excitement moves you forward.

- Fear holds you back.

Instead of letting emotions control you, learn to direct them. Use frustration as fuel. Convert excitement into execution. Master this, and you master life.

4. Emotion = Energy in Motion

Ever noticed how emotions can make you feel stuck or unstoppable? That's because emotion is just energy in motion.

When you suppress emotions, that energy gets blocked. But when you express and channel them in the right way, they become a force that propels you forward.

Let your emotions move you—but always in the direction of growth.

5. Intuition Works Faster Than Intelligence

Your brain loves analyzing everything, but sometimes, it's too slow.

Ever had a gut feeling about something, and later, you realized you were right? That's intuition. It's faster than logic because it doesn't need step-by-step processing—it just knows.

The more you trust it, the more effortless your decisions become.

6. Fate, Destiny, and Free Will—The Formula for Life

Here's a simple way to look at it:

- Fate is the result of your past actions.

- Destiny is where those results are leading.

- Free Will is your power to change both—right now.

Think of it like a road.

- Fate is where you're standing.

- Destiny is where the road leads.

- Free will is your ability to take a new turn at any moment.

And what decides where you go? Your habits. They are the GPS guiding your journey.

7. Everything Around You Has a Pattern

Nothing in life is random. Success, failure, happiness, struggle—they all have patterns.

Instead of asking, Why is this happening to me? ask, What is the pattern here?

The moment you see the pattern, you gain the power to change it.

8. The Golden Message for the Golden Era

Here's something deep—every thought in your mind is a signal from the universe.

- Some thoughts guide you.

- Some thoughts test you.

- Some thoughts are just noise.

Your job? Learn to tell the difference.

9. Align Yourself with the Flow of Life

Growth isn't about force—it's about flow.

When you resist, you struggle. When you align, life becomes effortless.

A river doesn't fight to flow forward—it just moves with the path ahead. Your growth should be the same.

10. Trust the Process—Let Growth Happen Automatically

You don't need to control every detail of life. Just like a seed doesn't force itself to grow—it simply finds the right soil, gets enough sunlight, and transforms into a tree.

Your life is the same. Set the right conditions, and growth will take care of itself.

Now, if growth can be so effortless, why not make it completely automatic?

That's exactly what we'll talk about next: Why You Must Automate Your Growth.

4. Why You Must Automate Your Growth

My friend, let's talk about growth. Most people believe that personal and professional growth requires constant struggle—strategies, to-do lists, strict routines. And yes, they work... for a while.

But then what happens? Exhaustion. Inconsistency. Burnout.

That's because forcing growth is like trying to push a river—it goes against the natural flow of life. The more you struggle, the more resistance you create. But what if growth could happen effortlessly?

What if, instead of forcing yourself to grow, you could set things up so that growth happens on its own?

That's what automating your growth is all about.

Why Should You Automate Growth?

Because that's how nature works.

Look around you. A tree doesn't need reminders to grow. The sun doesn't hesitate before rising. Your body breathes without you thinking about it. Growth is not forced—it happens naturally when the right conditions are set.

But most people try to control and micromanage their growth, constantly adjusting and pushing themselves. That takes a lot of energy. Eventually, they burn out or give up.

Automation removes that struggle. It makes growth natural, predictable, and effortless.

What Happens When Growth is Automated?

The moment you automate your growth, you experience three powerful shifts:

- You save time and energy – A simple daily habit help complex strategies simple and effortless-driven self-improvement.

- You achieve consistency – Growth is no longer a fight; it becomes a natural part of your life.

- You live authentically – You stop forcing change and start evolving in a way that aligns with your true self.

But let me be clear—automation is not about becoming a machine. It's about creating a flow where success and growth happen effortlessly, just like breathing.

When you tap into the power of your superconscious mind, you don't need to force success—you become the kind of person for whom success happens naturally.

How Does This Book Help You Automate Growth?

Through a simple, yet powerful method.

Just 12 minutes a day is enough to activate an internal mechanism that drives your growth automatically.

- No information overload

- No excessive effort

- Just a shift in awareness that changes how you operate

When your inner world transforms, your thoughts, decisions, and actions naturally align with your highest potential.

Effortless, Sustainable, and Joyful Growth

The goal is not to make you work harder. It's to free you from unnecessary complexity. To make growth something that happens on its own—exactly when and where you need it, without you having to chase it.

"Automate Your Growth" isn't just a process—it's a lifestyle.

A way of trusting yourself, unlocking your hidden potential, and succeeding with freedom, joy, and authenticity.

Because when growth is automated, you don't just grow—you thrive.

And the secret to making this work? Understanding the power of alignment.

Let's explore that next: The Power of Alignment: Intellect as Your Compass.

5. The Power of Alignment: Intellect as Your Compass

My friend, imagine living a life where...

- Your mind is clear—no unnecessary thoughts weighing you down.

- You take action instantly, without hesitation or overthinking.

- Your emotions fuel your progress instead of holding you back.

- Your intuition leads you to the right choices effortlessly.

- You understand the forces of fate, destiny, and free will—and use them to shape your future.

If you could master just these things, growth wouldn't be something you chase—it would happen naturally, just like breathing.

That's the secret. That's how you automate your growth.

The Only Thing You Should Ask For

If there's one request we should make to the universal power, it's this:

"Guide my intellect in the right direction."

That's it.

Not asking for success.

Not praying for an easier life.

Not hoping for shortcuts.

Just this one simple request. Because when your intellect is aligned, everything else follows—your decisions, your actions, your results.

Your Intellect is Your Life's Compass

Think of your intellect as a compass. If it's pointing true north, you'll always move in the right direction. But if it's even slightly off?

You'll wander.

You'll make mistakes.

You'll struggle.

You'll wonder why life feels so difficult.

Most people ask for wealth, happiness, or success. But here's the truth—what's the point of having all that if you don't know how to handle it?

That's why the real ask should always be:

"Let my intellect be sharp, clear, and aligned with the highest truth."

Because when your intellect is aligned, growth happens effortlessly.

How This One Shift Changes Everything

When your intellect is in tune with truth and clarity:

- You stop wasting energy on unnecessary thoughts.

- You don't get stuck in emotions that slow you down.

- You avoid distractions and confusion.

- You take the right actions at the right time.

It's like activating autopilot for your life. You don't have to force growth—it happens on its own.

The Hidden Power of Intellect

Your intellect within your mind serves as the signal point of super consciousness, acting as a bridge between your true self (super consciousness) and your world (your body, mind, and surroundings)

- If that bridge is weak, your thoughts and actions stay disconnected—you keep wanting change, but nothing happens.

- If that bridge is strong, everything aligns—your thoughts turn into actions, and your actions turn into results.

That's why, instead of asking for external things, ask for:

- The wisdom to see clearly.

- The strength to choose wisely.

- The alignment to flow effortlessly with life.

When your intellect is clear, the universe takes care of the rest. Growth becomes automatic, success feels natural, and life turns into a beautiful, effortless journey.

That's the real secret, my friend.

Just one simple ask—and everything else follows.

Next: How to Align Your Intellect for Effortless Growth

6. How to Align Your Intellect for Effortless Growth

My friend, let me share something that might just change the way you see life forever.

Most of us believe we're in control—that we're the ones making decisions, shaping our future, and struggling to create success. But the truth? Life is predesigned. It already has a rhythm, a flow, a pattern.

The only real question is—are you aware of it?

Let's break this down.

1. Your World = Your Body, Mind, and Surroundings

Your entire experience of life exists in three dimensions:

- Your body – Your physical form, constantly moving through time.

- Your mind – The space where thoughts, emotions, and decisions arise.

- Your surroundings – The external world influencing your journey.

Now, here's the twist—none of these are fully in your control. They are being activated by something far greater than you.

2. The Universe Sends You Signals That Shape Your Reality

You are not separate from the universe. You are part of it. And it constantly sends you signals—small nudges, insights, moments of clarity.

Everything that happens to you—good, bad, or neutral—is a result of these signals. They are not random. They come from an infinite intelligence that guides your life's design.

The question is: Are you receiving them?

3. Your Intellect is Already Following a Predesigned Flow

Here's something mind-blowing—your intellect isn't random. It is part of a larger design, receiving and processing the universal signals.

So even when you think you're making independent choices, your intellect is actually working within boundaries set by the signals it receives.

4. Perception, Decisions, and Comparisons Happen Automatically

Every time you:

- Compare two choices

- Make a decision

- See the world a certain way

It's not just you doing it—it's the result of the signals entering your intellect.

This means:

- Your worldview is shaped by what the universal intelligence allows you to see.

- Your decisions are influenced by the signals you are receiving.

- Even the comparisons your mind makes are part of a grand, automatic process.

Most people don't realize this. They keep fighting life, trying to force things to happen. But those who do see it? They stop struggling. They start flowing.

5. Life Runs Automatically—But Only a Few Recognize It

Here's the biggest revelation: Everything in life is happening automatically.

Most people resist this truth. They struggle, thinking they must "control" everything. But those who awaken to it?

They let go.

They trust the flow.

And suddenly, life starts working for them instead of against them.

6. Creation, Sustenance, and Destruction Follow a Universal Schedule

Nothing in this universe happens randomly.

Everything—including people, opportunities, and even your thoughts—follows a timing cycle of:

- Creation – The birth of new experiences.

- Sustenance – Growth, stability, and evolution.

- Destruction – The natural end of phases to make way for the new.

When you truly understand this, you stop fearing endings, because you know they're just part of the process.

7. Free Will Exists—But It Operates Within the Grand Design

Now, you might be wondering—"If everything is predesigned, where does free will fit in?"

Yes, you have free will—you can choose, act, and shape your experience.

But here's the catch: The very capacity to use your free will—your energy, inspiration, and opportunities—comes from the collective intelligence of the universe.

So while you are free to choose, your ability to choose is still connected to the grand design.

8. Seeing Everything as One with the Super Consciousness

When you understand this deeply, something magical happens:

- Self-doubt disappears – Because you know you are already part of something bigger.

- Fear fades away – Because you trust the universal intelligence guiding your path.

- You stop chasing – Instead, you open yourself to receiving at the right time.

This is the ultimate state of effortless growth—where you are fully present, fully aware, and fully aligned with the flow of existence.

Align, Don't Resist

So, my friend, the only thing you truly need to do is this:

Let go of unnecessary resistance. Trust the signals. Align yourself with the higher intelligence guiding your path.

If there's just one idea you take from this, let it be this:

"Our life is predesigned, and the signals from collective intelligence work through every intellect to shape the world we see."

Once you truly grasp this, life no longer feels like a struggle. It becomes a beautifully orchestrated experience, where everything unfolds at the perfect time.

And when you see it this way, growth becomes automatic.

But even when you understand this, there are still obstacles— mental, emotional, and situational— that can hold you back.

That's why next, we'll talk about Breaking Barriers: Overcoming Obstacles to Growth.

7. Breaking Barriers: Overcoming Obstacles to Growth

My friend, let's have a real conversation. Growth is exciting, but let's be honest—it's not always easy. It feels like we're constantly running into invisible walls, doesn't it?

One moment, we're motivated and ready to change, and the next, we're stuck in the same patterns, wondering why nothing is shifting. But what if I told you that these barriers aren't just random obstacles? What if they are signals—pointing us toward the exact lessons we need to master?

Let's dive into the common roadblocks that hold us back and, more importantly, how we can move past them with ease.

The Hardest Battle: Facing Yourself

Turning inward—really looking at yourself—is one of the most challenging yet rewarding things you'll ever do. Why? Because it forces you to confront things you might have been avoiding for years.

Why It Feels So Difficult:

Fear of What You'll Find: We're afraid we might not like what we see—old wounds, insecurities, regrets.

Distraction is Easier: It's simpler to focus on external achievements, social media, or work than to sit alone with our thoughts.

The World is Noisy: Silence feels foreign when we're constantly bombarded with distractions.

How to Overcome It:

- Start Small – Just five minutes of stillness each day can change your life. Whether it's journaling, meditating, or simply taking a deep breath, these moments create clarity.

- Observe Without Judgment – Instead of labeling your thoughts as 'good' or 'bad,' just notice them. Awareness is the first step to transformation.

- Trust the Process – The discomfort of self-reflection is temporary. The longer you avoid it, the longer you stay stuck.

The truth? The moment you stop running from yourself and start observing, you gain the power to grow effortlessly.

Breaking Free from Repeating Patterns

Have you ever noticed how certain thoughts and behaviors seem to be on a loop? Procrastination, self-doubt, blaming others, limiting beliefs—they're like autopilot programs running in the background. But here's the liberating truth: they're not YOU. They're just habits. And habits can be changed.

How to Break Free:

Spot the Pattern – Start noticing the thoughts that hold you back. Journaling helps with this.

Challenge the Narrative – When a limiting belief pops up, question it. Instead of "I can't do this," ask, "What if I can?"

Take Small Actions – One small, intentional step today rewires your brain for change.

Surround Yourself with Positivity – Engage with people and resources that uplift you instead of reinforcing old patterns.

Growth isn't about making a massive leap overnight. It's about choosing new patterns over old ones, consistently, until transformation becomes second nature.

The Secret to Lasting Happiness

Most people spend their lives chasing happiness—believing it comes from success, possessions, or validation from others. But here's the thing: anything external can be taken away. Real happiness? That comes from within.

Why External Happiness Fails:

- It's fleeting and dependent on circumstances.

- Seeking validation from others leads to insecurity and anxiety.

- When expectations aren't met, disappointment follows.

How to Cultivate Inner Happiness:

- Practice Gratitude – Even on the hardest days, there's something to be thankful for. Gratitude shifts your focus from lack to abundance.

- Live Authentically – Stop living for what others expect. Align with what truly matters to you.

- Be Present – The mind loves to dwell on the past or worry about the future. But joy? It's always in the NOW.

When happiness comes from within, you become unshakable. Life's ups and downs no longer control you—you navigate them with ease and confidence.

Growth Becomes Effortless

Overcoming obstacles isn't about fighting them—it's about understanding them. The moment you stop fearing self-reflection, break free from negative patterns, and anchor your happiness within, growth happens naturally. It stops being a struggle and starts feeling like a beautifully unfolding journey.

And this leads us to the next big revelation—how growth can happen on autopilot. Imagine a life where transformation is not forced but automatic, where success, joy, and clarity come effortlessly. Sounds incredible, doesn't it?

Next, Let's explore how that works! We will see it in the "Ultimate Outcome: Growth on Autopilot".

8. The Ultimate Outcome: Growth on Autopilot

My friend, imagine a life where you no longer struggle to grow. No forcing yourself into routines, no chasing after success with endless effort. Instead, growth happens naturally—like breathing.

This isn't some distant dream. It's the ultimate outcome when you align yourself with the right principles, develop clarity, and take actions in tune with your true self.

You don't have to keep "fixing" yourself. You don't have to push through obstacles with sheer willpower every single day. You simply become the kind of person for whom growth is effortless.

How is that possible? Let me break it down for you.

When Growth Becomes Automatic

Think about it—does a tree force itself to grow? Does a river struggle to flow toward the ocean? No. Growth is the most natural thing in the universe. It only feels hard when we resist it.

But the moment we align our intellect, emotions, and actions with our authentic self, growth starts to happen without conscious effort.

Here's what changes when you reach this state:

- Decisions Become Instinctive: You no longer overthink every move. Your intellect is so sharp and aligned that you just know what needs to be done.

- Effort Feels Effortless: You take action—not out of stress or fear, but because it feels natural and exciting. Work becomes play. Challenges become stepping stones.

- Obstacles Don't Drain You: You stop resisting life. Instead of reacting to problems with frustration, you respond with wisdom. Setbacks don't derail you because you trust the process.

- Happiness Flows From Within: You no longer depend on external factors to feel fulfilled. Your joy isn't tied to achievements or circumstances. It comes from a deep sense of alignment.

- You Feel Guided, Always: No more confusion. No more hesitation. You sense the right direction and move forward with confidence.

In short, growth becomes as natural as breathing.

The Real Secret: You Don't "Do" Growth. You "Become" Growth.

At this point, you might be wondering: But how do I actually reach this state?

The answer is simple: By being consistent with small, daily actions.

Big transformations don't come from massive, one-time efforts. They come from the tiny habits you repeat every single day.

And that, my friend, is the perfect bridge to our next chapter: Habit.

If growth is the goal, habit is the mechanism that makes it happen automatically. The habits you cultivate determine whether you stay stuck or evolve effortlessly.

So let's dive in and uncover a 12-minute daily habit that turn your growth into a permanent, unstoppable force.

9. Summary of the Chapter

The Universe is on Autopilot—So is Life

Just like the universe follows a natural rhythm—planets orbit, seasons change, and rivers flow effortlessly—our lives can also operate on autopilot. The key to effortless growth is not force but alignment. The reason we struggle with overthinking, inconsistency, and procrastination is resistance. But when we automate our growth, life flows smoothly, just like the universe.

Life's Grand Design: The Balance of Free Will and Destiny

Life operates on a predesigned script, yet we still have free will. Imagine destiny as a river—it has a direction, but you decide how you navigate it. You can fight against the current or flow with it. The secret to growth is using your free will to align with life's natural design rather than resisting it.

The Foundation of Automated Growth

Growth doesn't have to be a struggle. A tree doesn't force itself to grow; it just finds the right conditions. The same applies to personal development. To automate growth:

- Think Less – Overthinking creates resistance; action creates momentum.

- Take Action Instantly – Reduce hesitation and act without doubt.

- Use Emotions as Energy – Emotions fuel action; direct them wisely.

- Trust Intuition – Your inner wisdom is faster than logic.

- Align with Patterns – Success follows patterns; recognize and align with them.

Why You Must Automate Your Growth

Growth should be effortless, just like breathing. When growth is automated:

- You save time and energy.

- You stay consistent without relying on motivation.

- You evolve in a way that feels natural.

The book introduces a 12-minute daily habit that shifts your awareness and transforms your life without excessive effort.

The Power of Alignment: Intellect as Your Compass

Your intellect is the compass that determines your life's direction. If misaligned, life feels like a struggle. If aligned, growth happens naturally. Instead of asking for wealth or success, the most powerful request to the universe is:

"Guide my intellect in the right direction."

When your intellect is aligned, you think clearly, act decisively, and flow effortlessly with life.

How to Align Your Intellect for Effortless Growth

Life operates through universal signals that guide your journey. Recognizing and following these signals eliminates struggle. The realization that life runs on a predesigned flow allows you to trust the process and stop resisting. True transformation happens when you align yourself with this natural rhythm.

Breaking Barriers: Overcoming Obstacles to Growth

The biggest roadblock to growth is resistance—fear, overthinking, and repeating patterns. To break free:

- Face Yourself – Self-awareness is the first step.

- Break Old Patterns – Identify and replace limiting beliefs.

- Anchor Happiness Within – External success is temporary; real happiness is internal.

The Ultimate Outcome: Growth on Autopilot

When growth is automated:

- Decisions become effortless.

- Success feels natural.

- Obstacles no longer drain you.

- You feel guided and in flow with life.

The goal is not to force change but to become the kind of person for whom growth is automatic.

What's Next?

The chapter sets the stage for the next big idea: Habit—the mechanism that makes growth automatic. A simple, structured 12-minute daily habit can rewire your mind, align your intellect, and make success a natural part of your life.

Chapter 2

Habit

1. Habits: The Unseen Force Shaping Your Future

Hey my friend, let me tell you something that might change the way you see your life—you don't directly create your future.

Your habits do.

Think about it. The things you do every single day, even the smallest ones, are quietly shaping your future. You don't suddenly wake up successful, healthy, or happy by accident. It happens because of the habits you've built—consciously or unconsciously—over time.

And here's the best part: your habits are completely in your control. No one else can decide them for you. Every action you repeat is a step in some direction—either toward the life you want or away from it.

So, let's pause for a moment. Ask yourself:

- Where are my habits leading me?

- If I keep doing what I'm doing today, where will I be in a year? Five years?

If you like the answer, great—keep going. If you don't, then it's time to change your habits. Because your future isn't some mysterious force—it's being built right now, one small action at a time. So choose wisely.

Are We Creating Our Future, or Is It Already Designed?

Alright, let's go a little deeper.

You now know that your habits shape your future, but what about destiny? If everything is pre-designed, then does it even matter what you do?

Here's something interesting to think about—when an opportunity comes your way, and you have the free will to act on it, doesn't that show that something bigger than you is working in your favor?

Think about all the times life has nudged you in a certain direction—those coincidences, those unexpected breakthroughs, the moments when things just "click." That's not random. It's as if the universe—this vast intelligence—is guiding you, opening doors, and waiting to see if you step through.

Now, if someone doesn't believe in this principle, they would have to create countless theories to explain every so-called coincidence, every challenge, every unexpected insight. But the truth is much simpler.

Your mind and intellect do not function in isolation; they are connected to something far greater—whether you call it super consciousness, universal power, or collective intelligence.

Ever wondered where a thought comes from? Why some ideas feel like sudden sparks of inspiration? Your mind isn't just a machine processing information—it's a receiver. It taps into a larger intelligence that constantly feeds you insights, ideas, and guidance.

But here's the catch—this intelligence won't take action for you.

The universe can give you opportunities, but only your habits determine whether you make the most of them. The knowledge, the wisdom, the insights—they're all there. But what you do with them? That's entirely up to you.

So trust the process. Align yourself with the wisdom that flows through you. And take responsibility for shaping your own path. Because when your free will aligns with universal intelligence, that's when you create a future worth living.

And now, my friend, the next question is: how do you consciously design habits that work for you, not against you?

That's exactly what we'll dive into next—Harnessing the Power of Intentional Habits. Let's go.

2. Harnessing the Power of Intentional Habits

Hello friend, have you ever realized how much of your life runs on autopilot? The way you wake up, the way you react to challenges, the way you spend your time—it's all shaped by habits, whether you're aware of it or not.

But here's the real question: Are your habits working for you or against you?

There's a huge difference between habits that sneak into your life without your awareness and intentional habits that you consciously design to align with your highest goals. And the secret to unstoppable growth? It's not just having habits—it's about building them on purpose.

Let's break it down.

The Science Behind Habits

Neuroscience tells us that habits are simply patterns formed through repetition. The more you repeat an action, the stronger the neural pathway in your brain, until it eventually becomes automatic.

- Passive Habits: These are habits that form unconsciously—often working against your best interests. Think about how easily you scroll through social media or procrastinate when facing something challenging.

- Intentional Habits: These are habits you consciously design to serve your growth. They may take effort at first, but with consistency, they become second nature—just like brushing your teeth.

Lesson: The more intentional you are with your habits, the more you automate your growth instead of leaving it to chance.

Why Intentional Habits Matter

Ever wonder why some people seem to achieve their goals effortlessly while others struggle even though they work hard? It's not luck. It's alignment.

When you build habits with intention:

Your Actions Align with Your Purpose – You stop drifting and start moving deliberately toward your vision.

You Reduce Decision Fatigue – Automating positive behaviors frees up mental energy for bigger, more meaningful decisions.

You Build Momentum – Small, consistent actions compound over time, leading to massive growth.

You Strengthen Your Authenticity – When your habits reflect your values, you feel more centered and confident in who you are.

Lesson: Growth isn't about working harder—it's about working smarter, with purpose.

How to Build Intentional Habits That Stick

Good news: You don't need a total life overhaul. Small, simple steps lead to lasting change.

1. Start Small

Pick one habit that takes just a couple of minutes a day. The easier it is, the more likely you'll stick with it.

2. Be Consistent

Even five minutes a day is more powerful than an hour once a week. Consistency beats intensity.

3. Anchor It to an Existing Routine

Want to start meditating? Do it right after brushing your teeth. Want to practice gratitude? Do it while sipping your morning coffee.

4. Focus on the Process, Not Just the Outcome

Success isn't just about the result—it's about who you become through the process. Trust the journey.

5. Track Your Progress

Use a simple checklist, journal, or app to reinforce your commitment. Small wins create big momentum.

Lesson: Don't overwhelm yourself with big changes overnight. Master small habits first, and let them grow.

The Power of the 12-Minute Daily Practice

So, what's the easiest way to integrate intentional habits into your life? By making them part of a structured, non-negotiable daily practice.

Here's how you can transform your life in just 12 minutes a day: Spend one minute each on the following areas to build a habit that drives lasting transformation:

Sound – Tune in to the subtle sound beyond the noise, the hum of existence.

Light – See the inner light within you, a source of clarity and wisdom.

Body – Acknowledge and appreciate your physical being.

Breath – Observe your natural breath, without controlling it.

Mind – Witness your thoughts without judgment.

Intellect – Recognize the part of you that analyzes and interprets.

Memory – Acknowledge its vast power to store and retrieve.

Ego – Observe the identity you create for yourself.

True Self – Go beyond body and mind to recognize the real YOU.

Present Moment – Shift your awareness to NOW, where life truly happens.

Purify – Use this light to cleanse negativity and heal from within.

Thank –the universal energy for Intentions, gratitude and blessings

The beauty of this practice? It's simple, flexible, and powerful. You can do it in the morning, before bed, or even during a break. The key is consistency.

Overcoming Common Barriers

"I don't have time."

12 minutes is just 1% of your day. If your growth isn't worth 1%, what is?

"I don't feel motivated."

Motivation is fleeting. But discipline? That's what keeps you going.

"I missed a day. Now what?"

Missing one day is fine. Missing two in a row? That's a pattern. Just get back on track—without guilt.

Lesson: Your commitment matters more than perfection.

The Ripple Effect of Intentional Habits

Once you integrate intentional habits into your daily life, the impact goes far beyond just those 12 minutes:

- You'll approach challenges with more clarity and confidence.

- Your daily actions will naturally align with your bigger goals.

- You'll feel more centered, authentic, and fulfilled.

Intentional habits are like planting seeds. Give them time. Nurture them daily. And watch them grow into something extraordinary.

The Practice of Integration

Here's what I want you to take away, my friend:

The 12-minute practice isn't just another habit—it's a transformative daily ritual. It keeps you connected to your true self, aligns your actions with your purpose, and automates your growth.

Start small. Stay consistent. And let the power of intentional habits shape your journey toward your best self.

Your 12 minutes start now. Are you ready?

And now, let's dive into something even more exciting—why just 12 minutes a day can completely transform your life. Let's go.

3. Why 12 Minutes Can Transform Your Life

Hey my friend, let me ask you something—what if just 12 minutes a day could completely change your life?

I know, I know—it sounds almost too simple, right? We're so used to thinking that big results require massive effort, endless hours, and a complete life overhaul. But what if the opposite were true? What if small, consistent actions could create unstoppable momentum?

This is exactly why I emphasize a 12-minute daily practice. It's short enough to fit into even the busiest schedule, yet powerful enough to rewire your mind, strengthen your habits, and unlock unstoppable growth.

Let's break it down.

Why 12 Minutes?

You might be wondering, "Why 12 minutes? Why not 30? Why not an hour?"

Here's the thing—most personal growth routines fail because they demand too much time and effort. They feel overwhelming. And let's be honest, when something feels like a burden, it's only a matter of time before we drop it.

But 12 minutes? That's different. It's the sweet spot—short enough to be doable, long enough to be meaningful.

Think of it like a drop of water. A single drop seems insignificant, but when it drips consistently, it can carve through stone. That's the power of 12 minutes—small, daily efforts that create a lasting impact.

The Science Behind Small, Consistent Actions

Psychology and neuroscience both tell us the same thing: consistency rewires your brain. Every time you repeat an action, you strengthen the neural pathways associated with it. Eventually, that action becomes second nature.

Even just 12 minutes a day can:

Activate Your Brain's Focus – Short bursts of intentional practice improve clarity and decision-making.

Build Momentum – When something feels easy to start, you're less likely to procrastinate.

Create Compounding Growth – Just like compound interest, small daily efforts add up to massive transformation over time.

Lesson: It's not what you do once in a while that shapes your life—it's what you do every single day.

Why Not More Time?

Now, you might be thinking, "If 12 minutes is good, wouldn't an hour be better?"

Not necessarily. The problem with long, demanding routines is that they're hard to maintain.

- They feel like a chore – And the moment something feels like work, we resist it.

- They drain energy instead of creating it – If you're exhausted after a long session, you won't stick with it.

- They lead to burnout – And burnout leads to inconsistency, which is the biggest killer of progress.

But 12 minutes?

- It fits into any schedule – Morning, lunch break, before bed— whenever works for you.

- It keeps you engaged – A short, focused session is more impactful than a long, distracted one.

- It fuels you, not drains you – Instead of taking away energy, it gives you more.

Lesson: It's not about doing more—it's about doing enough, consistently.

The Power of Focused Intention

Here's what really makes those 12 minutes powerful—it's not just the time itself, but how you use it.

When you dedicate 12 minutes to your growth, you're not just passing time. You're:

- Aligning with your purpose – So your daily actions match your long-term vision.

- Cultivating gratitude and clarity – So you start each day with the right mindset.

- Strengthening your authentic self – So you grow in alignment with your true values.

- Focusing on what truly matters – So your energy is spent on what moves you forward.

This practice becomes a reset button—keeping you centered, focused, and in control of your life.

Lesson: Even a few minutes of focused effort can shift your entire mindset.

A Symbolic Commitment to Growth

Beyond practicality, 12 minutes carries deep meaning.

It's a promise to yourself – That you're serious about your growth.

It proves that change is possible – No matter how busy you are.

It builds self-trust – Because when you show up for yourself daily, you strengthen your confidence.

Lesson: Dedicating just 12 minutes to growth sends a powerful message to yourself: "I am committed to becoming my best self."

The Long-Term Impact of Just 12 Minutes a Day

Still not sure? Let's look at the compounding effect.

- One Week In – You'll feel more clear-headed, focused, and intentional.

- One Month In – You'll notice real shifts in your habits and mindset.

- One Year In – That's 73 hours of dedicated personal growth—enough to completely transform your life.

Lesson: It's not about how much time you spend in a day—it's about how consistently you invest in yourself.

Who Is This For?

The best part? Anyone can do this.

- Professionals.

- Leaders.

- Students.

- Anyone juggling personal and professional life.

You don't need expensive courses, fancy tools, or a complete life overhaul—just 12 minutes and the willingness to grow.

The Real Question: Are You Ready?

So, let me ask you again:

Can 12 minutes a day change your life?

The real question isn't whether you have 12 minutes—it's whether you're willing to give yourself 12 minutes.

This simple, consistent practice is the foundation of Automate Your Growth. It helps you align your actions, build powerful habits, and unlock your true potential—all in just 12 minutes a day.

Growth doesn't have to feel like a struggle. It can be effortless, natural, and deeply transformative.

Your 12 minutes start now. Are you in?

Next Up: The 12 Key Elements of This Practice

Now that you understand the power of 12 minutes, you might be wondering—what exactly should you do in that time?

Great question. Let's break down the 12 key elements that make this practice truly life-changing...

4. The 12 Key Elements of This Practice

My friend, have you ever wondered what truly makes a habit life-changing?

It's not just about repeating an action—it's about what that action connects you to. A habit becomes powerful when it aligns with your energy, your purpose, and your true self. That's when it stops being just another routine and starts reshaping your life.

These 12 elements aren't just techniques; they're gateways to a richer, more conscious way of living. They help you tune into your mind, body, and spirit, so every day feels more aligned, powerful, and meaningful.

Let's explore them together.

1. Hear Your Sound: The Vibration of the Universe Within You

Friend, have you ever thought about how everything around us—literally everything—is vibrating? From the tiniest atom to the biggest galaxy, nothing is ever truly still. And here's the cool part: sound isn't just what you hear with your ears. It's the very frequency of existence itself.

Now, what if I told you that by simply listening—really listening—you could tune into the very heartbeat of the universe? Let's break it down:

1. Everything is Vibration

Science already confirms this. Every single thing—your body, your thoughts, even the device you're holding—is just energy vibrating at different frequencies. What feels "solid" is actually a dance of tiny moving particles.

Think about it: A ringing bell, the rustling of leaves, or even the quiet between sounds—it's all vibration.

2. The Universe Has Its Own Sound

Ancient wisdom and modern physics both hint that the universe itself has a resonance, a hum, a frequency.

And get this—you don't have to "make" a sound to experience it. You just have to listen.

Ever noticed? The wind passing through trees, the distant sound of waves, or even complete silence—it all carries presence.

3. Deep Listening Connects You to the Infinite

Here's where it gets profound. When you listen without analyzing, without interrupting with your own thoughts, you actually become one with that universal vibration. That's why meditation, chanting, or simply sitting in deep silence can feel so powerful.

Ever wonder why? Monks and sages practice deep listening— not just to hear, but to tune in to something beyond words.

So How Does This All Come Together?

- Everything vibrates → The universe itself is a sound

- You don't have to create sound → Just listen to the presence of vibration

- Deep listening → Connects you to something infinite

Try This:

Close your eyes, take a deep breath, and hum softly. Feel that vibration moving through your body. That's not just sound—it's energy, grounding you, aligning you.

Why it matters: The right sound—whether a mantra, music, or the natural hum of existence—can reset your mind and soul. It's not just noise; it's pure energy in motion.

And if sound is vibration, guess what? Light is vibration too. But instead of hearing it, you see it.

Let's talk about that next: See Your Light.

2. See Your Light: The Focus of Universal Consciousness

Friend, have you ever thought about the light within you? I'm not talking about the light you see with your eyes—I mean the pure awareness that's always present, always watching, always you.

This inner light isn't something you have to search for outside. It's been there all along. The moment you see it, you experience a deep sense of peace, clarity, and connection with everything. Let's break it down:

1. Consciousness is the Source of Awareness

Think about it—your thoughts, emotions, and even your body all exist within your awareness. But what's behind all of them? Who's the one noticing your thoughts?

That's your pure consciousness. It's the silent observer. The real you. And guess what? That's the light within.

2. Your Inner Light is Beyond Thoughts & Judgments

Your mind is always busy—analyzing, comparing, making up stories. But what happens when you step back and just observe? No judgments, no opinions—just being.

Try this: Sit quietly for a moment. Don't think, don't label, don't even try to "meditate." Just notice that you exist. That's your inner light shining.

3. Recognizing Your Light Brings Oneness

Here's the powerful part—when you see your inner light, you start seeing it in everyone. You realize that underneath all the noise, all the differences, there is a shared consciousness.

That's why enlightened beings radiate peace. They're not different from us—they've just become fully aware of their own inner light.

How It All Comes Together

- Your consciousness = Your inner light → It's always been there.

- Observing this light = No thoughts, no judgments → Just pure presence.

- This presence connects you to the universe → Peace, clarity, oneness.

Try This:

Close your eyes for a few seconds. Imagine a warm, golden light inside you. Let it expand, filling every part of your being. Breathe into it. That light? That's you.

Why it matters: No matter how dark life feels sometimes, light is always within you. See it. Feel it. Live it.

And you know what carries this light? Your body. Let's talk about that next: Acknowledge Your Body.

3. Acknowledge Your Body: Your Living Instrument of Experience

Friend, have you ever stopped to really feel your body—not just when something aches or feels off, but just to appreciate it? Your body isn't just a machine carrying you around. It's a living, breathing, intelligent system working for you, every single moment. And most of the time? We take it for granted—until something goes wrong.

But what if we paid attention before that? Let's break it down:

1. Your Body is a Living System

Right now, without you even thinking about it, your heart is beating, your lungs are breathing, and your cells are regenerating. Your body is a self-regulating genius, constantly keeping you alive and balanced.

Think about it: You don't have to "remind" yourself to breathe or tell your stomach to digest food—it just happens. Your body knows what to do.

2. Attention to Your Body Boosts Energy & Awareness

Here's something fascinating: When you bring awareness to your body, it responds. A simple smile releases energy that travels through your entire system. Tuning in to your body even for a few moments can boost your vitality.

Try this: Close your eyes, smile softly, and feel each part of your body. You'll notice an instant shift—a sense of calm, a little spark of energy.

3. Your Body is Your Connection to the World

Every experience you've ever had—every hug, every step, every moment of joy—happened through your body. It's how you see, touch, move, listen, and express yourself.

Imagine this: Without your body, you wouldn't be able to dance to your favorite song, feel the warmth of sunlight, or hold someone's hand. It's your bridge to life itself.

So, What's the Big Picture?

- Your body is a living system → Always working to support you.

- Acknowledging it fuels energy & well-being → The more you listen, the better it functions.

- It's your point of contact with life → The way you experience everything.

Try This:

Right now, feel your feet on the ground. Notice your heartbeat. Pay attention to the rhythm of your breath. And just say, "Thank you, body."

Why it matters: The more you respect and care for your body, the more it supports you in everything you do. It's not just a vessel—it's your greatest ally in this journey of life.

And speaking of your body... the breath is what keeps it all going. Let's explore that next: Enjoy Your Breath.

4. Enjoy Your Breath: The Key to Energy, Balance & Joy

Friend, have you ever noticed how you're breathing *right now*? Probably not, right? That's the thing—your breath is always there, quietly keeping you alive, yet we barely pay attention to it. But here's the secret: the way you breathe can *completely* change the way you feel—your energy, your emotions, even your thoughts.

Let's dive in:

1. Breath Fuels Your Body & Mind

Every single cell in your body runs on oxygen. The better you breathe, the more energy and clarity you have. But when we're stressed or distracted, our breathing becomes shallow—giving our body just enough to get by, but never enough to truly thrive.

Try this: The next time you feel drained, take three slow, deep breaths. Feel the difference? That's oxygen waking you up from the inside out.

2. Your Breath Controls Your Emotions? (And Not the Other Way Around?)

Ever noticed how your breath changes with your mood?

- Stressed? Your breath becomes fast and shallow.

- Relaxed? It slows down, deep and steady.

Here's the cool part: this works both ways. You don't just breathe because you're anxious—your anxious breathing makes you feel anxious! But when you slow your breath, your nervous system calms down, and suddenly, everything feels more manageable.

Example: Taking a few deep breaths before a big meeting or presentation helps you feel instantly more confident and in control.

3. Observing Your Breath Creates a Natural Flow

You don't always have to control your breath—sometimes, just watching it is enough. When you observe your breath, your mind settles, your body relaxes, and you naturally slip into a rhythm of peace and clarity.

Think about it: Meditation isn't about forcing thoughts away; it's just about watching your breath, letting it guide you into stillness.

How It All Comes Together

- Your breath fuels your body → More oxygen, more energy.

- Controlling your breath balances emotions → Less stress, more calm.

- Observing your breath creates awareness → A clearer, more joyful mind.

Try This:

Breathe in deeply for 4 seconds. Hold for 4. Exhale for 4. Feel the shift? That's your breath resetting you.

Why it matters: Your breath is always there, ready to bring you back to balance. Whenever life feels overwhelming, just return to it.

And speaking of balance—your breath and your mind are deeply connected. Let's explore that next: Accompany Your Mind.

5.Accompany Your Mind: From Wandering Thoughts to Conscious Awareness

Friend, have you ever noticed how your mind never really sits still? One second you're here, and the next, you're thinking about dinner, a past conversation, or some wild what-if scenario. It's like a browser with too many tabs open—constantly jumping between them. But what if, instead of letting your thoughts run you, you could simply walk with them—fully aware, fully present?

Let's break it down:

1. Your Mind is Always in Motion

Your mind is like a river—it flows non-stop. Some thoughts make sense, others feel random, and some completely take over. The tricky part? You don't choose most of them. They just show up.

Example: You're reading a book, and suddenly—boom—you're thinking about a conversation from last week, what to cook for dinner, or a meeting tomorrow. Sound familiar?

2. The Only Reality is the Present

Here's something crazy: The past is just a memory, and the future is just imagination. The only thing that's actually real is NOW. Your mind is most powerful when it's fully present in the moment.

Think about it: When you're deeply immersed in a sport, an art project, or a conversation, time disappears, right? That's because you're fully here, and that's where your mind is strongest.

3. Awareness is the Game-Changer

Most of the time, we don't even realize what our mind is doing. It's like we're being dragged along by thoughts without even noticing. But when you start observing your thoughts—without fighting them—you become aware of them.

This is mindfulness—seeing your thoughts without letting them control you.

Example: Instead of getting overwhelmed by stress, you step back and say, "Oh, that's stress. I see it. It's just a thought." And just like that, you loosen its grip.

How It All Comes Together

- Your mind moves constantly → But you don't have to follow every thought.

- The present is the only reality → The more aware you are, the more powerful you become.

- Awareness turns thoughts into wisdom → You stop reacting and start choosing.

Try This:

Next time a thought pops up—don't fight it. Just notice it and say, "I see you." Let it pass like a cloud in the sky.

Lesson: You are not your thoughts. You are the observer of them. The moment you start watching your mind instead of getting lost in it, you unlock a whole new level of clarity and freedom.

And speaking of clarity—there's a tool within you that helps you make sense of everything. Let's talk about it next: Recognize Your Intellect.

6. Recognize Your Intellect: The Bridge Between Mind, Body & Higher Intelligence

Ever feel like your mind is running in all directions while your body just follows along? That's where your intellect comes in—it's the decision-maker, the guide, the filter between random thoughts and wise action. Think of it as the captain of your inner ship, steering through the waves of emotions, thoughts, and experiences. But here's the real question: Are you using it wisely?

Let's break it down:

1. Your Intellect is the Command Center

Your body acts.

Your mind thinks and feels.

But your intellect? It decides what matters.

It sorts through emotions, thoughts, and impulses, helping you choose wisely instead of reacting blindly.

Example: Your mind might feel fear before speaking in public, but your intellect can analyze it, remind you of your preparation, and choose courage instead.

2. Intellect Helps You See Clearly

It's like a lens that helps you tell truth from illusion, wisdom from distraction.

Your mind might get caught up in overthinking, but your intellect steps in and says, "Wait, does this really matter?"

Example: Someone criticizes you. Your mind might feel hurt. But your intellect? It can decide whether to learn from it, ignore it, or respond calmly instead of reacting emotionally.

3. Intellect Connects You to Higher Intelligence

Your intellect isn't just a personal tool—it's also a receiver, like an antenna for wisdom.

When sharpened, it picks up insights, creativity, and solutions beyond your own experiences.

Example: Ever had a sudden brilliant idea out of nowhere? A deep realization that felt like it came from beyond your usual thoughts? That's your intellect tuning into something greater.

How It All Comes Together

- Your intellect processes thoughts → It guides your mind and body.

- It helps you see clearly → So you can make wise choices.

- It connects you to higher intelligence → Expanding your awareness and wisdom.

Try This:

Before making any decision, pause and ask: "Is this choice aligned with my values and long-term goals?"

Lesson: A strong intellect isn't about knowing everything—it's about knowing what truly matters.

And speaking of knowing—there's something even deeper that shapes our decisions: Our Memory. Let's dive into that next.

7.Realize Your Memory: The Storage & Retrieval System of Your Mind

Your memory is like an internal library—storing everything from childhood moments to yesterday's conversation. It shapes the way you think, react, and make decisions. But here's something we don't always realize: Memory doesn't work alone. It follows your intellect's guidance, deciding what to keep, what to forget, and how to use it. The question is—are you using your memory to grow or to stay stuck?

Let's break it down:

1. Your Memory is Like a Data Storage System

Think of your brain as a supercomputer. Every experience, thought, and feeling is recorded and stored. And guess what? These stored memories influence your choices, fears, and confidence.

Example: You remember past failures, so your mind hesitates before trying something new. It's like an old file being pulled up automatically.

2. Your Intellect Decides What Memory Stores

Not everything gets saved—your intellect acts as the filter, choosing what to keep and what to discard. If your intellect is cluttered with negativity, self-doubt, or distractions, memory follows that pattern. Example: If you keep saying, "I'm bad at public speaking," your memory will reinforce that belief by recalling only the moments you struggled, ignoring times you did well.

3. Memory's Potential is Unlimited

You can train your intellect to organize, refine, and reframe memories—just like cleaning up your phone storage to make space for what truly matters.

Example: If you practice gratitude daily, your brain will store more positive experiences, shaping a happier, more confident mindset.

How It All Comes Together

- Memory stores experiences → But your intellect decides what gets saved.

- Intellect can guide memory → Strengthening useful thoughts, discarding the noise.

- A trained intellect improves memory potential → Leading to clarity, growth, and better decisions.

Try This:

Think of a past mistake. Instead of feeling guilty, ask yourself:

"What did this teach me?" and move forward with wisdom.

Lesson: Memory is a tool, not a trap. Use it to learn and evolve, not to hold yourself back.

And speaking of things that shape us—let's talk about something even trickier: The Ego. What is it really, and how does it control us? Let's dive in.

8.Observe Your Ego: The Identity Trap of Body & Mind

Ever felt like you had to defend your opinion, prove your worth, or protect your image? That's your ego at work! It's the part of you that insists, "This is who I am!"—based on your body, mind, experiences, and what society has told you. But is that the real you? Let's break this down.

1. Your Ego Is Just a Mental Identity System

Think of your ego as your personal branding machine. It collects memories, beliefs, and social conditioning to build an identity.

It tells you:

- "I am an engineer."

- "I am introverted/extroverted."

- "I am smart, successful, or struggling."

But here's the catch—this is just a story your mind creates. Are you really just your profession, personality, or past experiences?

2. Your Ego Shapes How You Act

Because the ego believes you are your body and mind, it makes sure you act in ways that match that identity.

This influences:

- Your character (how you think)

- Your behavior (how you act)

- Your culture (how you relate to others)

Example: If you strongly identify as a "successful engineer," you might feel the need to constantly prove your intelligence or status—even when it's unnecessary.

3. Your Ego Filters How You See the World

You don't see reality as it is—you see it through the lens of your ego.

It creates:

- Judgments

- Comparisons

- Emotional reactions

Example: Someone questions your beliefs. Instead of considering their perspective, your ego jumps in—"They're attacking me!"—and suddenly, you feel defensive. But is that really you reacting? Or just your ego protecting its identity?

4. Observing Your Ego Sets You Free

The moment you observe your ego, you realize—it's just a mental construct, not your true self.

With awareness, you gain:

- Clarity (you stop reacting impulsively)

- Inner freedom (you see beyond your conditioned identity)

- Peace (because you no longer take everything personally)

How It All Connects:

- Your ego = your identity based on body & mind

- This identity shapes how you think, act, and perceive the world

- Observing your ego dissolves illusions → reveals your true self

Lesson: The ego seeks control; the true self seeks freedom. Choose wisely.

Here's something to try:

Next time you feel triggered, pause and ask: "Is this really me, or just my ego reacting?"

And that brings us to the next big question—if you're not your ego... then who are you? That's where Being Your Self comes in. Let's dive in.

9.Being Your Self: Beyond Body & Mind, Into Universal Connection

Have you ever wondered—Who am I, really? Most of us say, "I am my body" or "I am my mind." But if you take a step back, you'll realize something deeper... you are beyond both. When you let go of rigid labels and identities, you tap into something much bigger—an infinite intelligence that connects everything. Let's break this down.

1. You Are Not Just Your Body

Your body is always changing—new cells form, old ones die, your appearance evolves. But through all of this, you still feel like the same person.

So, here's the question—If you were only your body, who is the one watching all these changes happen?

2. You Are Not Just Your Mind

Your thoughts, emotions, and beliefs are like clouds in the sky—constantly shifting.

You might believe something strongly today and laugh at it years later.

So, if you were only your mind, what is that unchanging part of you that observes all these passing thoughts?

3. The True You Is Beyond Both

Once you stop identifying only with your body and mind, a powerful realization happens—you are part of something vast, something infinite.

This is what spiritual wisdom calls higher consciousness, universal intelligence, or the true self.

It's the space of deep clarity, peace, and limitless potential.

4. Becoming "Thou" – The Universal Principle

When you stop seeing yourself as just an individual and start flowing with the universal rhythm, something magical happens.

You no longer seek connection—you are connection.

You no longer struggle for clarity—you become clarity.

This is the ultimate state of being—where life moves through you, effortlessly.

How It All Connects:

- You observe your body—but you are not just your body.

- You watch your thoughts—but you are not just your mind.

- You are the pure awareness that is something far greater than your body and mind.

The more you embrace your true self, the more life flows effortlessly.

Here's something to try:

Spend a few moments alone, without distractions.

Ask yourself—"What truly excites me? What lights up my soul?"

That's where the real you begins.

And here's the key—once you tap into your true self, you don't need to fight with life anymore. Instead, you accept the present moment as it is, knowing that everything is unfolding for you. That's where we're headed next: Accept Your Present.

10. Accept Your Present: The Only Moment You Truly Live

Let me ask you something—where is life actually happening? Not in the past (that's just a memory). Not in the future (that's just imagination). Life is only happening right now. Yet, we spend so much time stuck in what was or what might be that we miss the only thing that's real—the present moment. Let's break this down.

1. The Present Is the Only Reality

Think about it:

- You can't change the past—it's already gone.

- You can't control the future—it's unknown.

- But right now? You can see, feel, act, and create.

This is the only time you are truly alive.

2. Free Will Exists Only in the Present

Ever noticed that all your decisions, actions, and choices only happen now?

You don't act in the past or the future—you act in the present.

The more you stay here, the more intentional and powerful your actions become.

3. Being Present Brings Clarity & Flow

When you fully absorb yourself in this moment:

- Your thoughts quiet down.

- You see things as they truly are, not as your mind projects them.

- You stop overthinking, and life starts flowing effortlessly.

Instead of getting lost in regrets (past) or worries (future), you feel peace—because you are actually here.

How It All Connects:

- Being present removes distractions → You act with clarity.

- Acting with clarity improves choices → Life becomes meaningful.

- Flowing with the moment reduces stress → You experience true peace.

- Accept your present. Live now. Flow freely. This is where life happens.

Here's something to try:

Throughout your day, pause and say, "I am here, in this moment."

Take a deep breath. Feel it fully. That's real life.

And here's the thing—when you're fully present, you start to notice something else. Your surroundings, your thoughts, your influences... they shape your experience. That's why the next step is Purify Your World—because what surrounds you, affects you. Let's explore.

11.Purify Your World: Body, Mind & Surroundings

Have you ever noticed how everything in your life—your energy, your thoughts, your mood—is influenced by what surrounds you? Your world isn't just what you see outside; it begins within—your body, your mind, and your environment. When these are pure and balanced, life feels lighter, clearer, and effortless. Let's break it down.

1. Purify Your Body → Release Pain, Gain Energy

Your body is your home—the foundation of everything you do. When you take care of it with good food, movement, and rest, you feel the difference.

- Eat clean, and your energy soars.

- Move your body, and stiffness melts away.

- Rest well, and clarity replaces exhaustion.

A pain-free, energized body allows you to fully live—not just exist.

2. Purify Your Mind → Clear Negative Thoughts, Invite Positivity

Ever had one negative thought spiral into a bad day? That's because your mind is like a garden—what you plant grows.

Fear, doubt, and anger? Weeds.

Kindness, clarity, and gratitude? Flowers.

When you consciously replace negativity with noble thoughts, you cleanse your mind. And a clear mind? It makes life so much smoother.

3. Purify Your Surroundings → Choose Noble Actions & Positive Company

Look around—your surroundings shape you more than you realize.

If your space is messy, your mind feels cluttered.

If you're surrounded by negativity, it drains your energy.

But when you create an environment filled with good people, uplifting actions, and simplicity, life feels peaceful and harmonious.

How It All Connects:

- A healthy body gives you the strength to think clearly.

- A clear mind helps you make positive choices.

- A positive environment reinforces good thoughts and actions.

When you purify all three, your world transforms into a place of peace, harmony, and joy.

Start small. Drink more water. Take deep breaths. Let go of toxic thoughts. Shift your space. Every little change purifies your world.

Try this:

Take a moment right now. Look around. Look within.

What's one thing you can cleanse today—your body, your thoughts, or your space? Start there.

And as you do, something incredible happens. You begin to feel gratitude—not just for things, but for your very existence. And that's where we're headed next: Thank Your Existence.

12.Thank Your Existence: The Power of Intentions, Blessings & Gratitude

Ever stopped to think about how incredible it is that you exist? That you—out of billions of possibilities—are here, thinking, feeling, experiencing? Your very existence is the root of everything: your intentions, the blessings you receive, and the gratitude you feel. Let's break this down.

1. Intentions Exist Because You Exist

Think about it—without existence, there would be no thoughts, no goals, no purpose. The very fact that you can dream, plan, and act comes from the foundation of simply being here.

Every time you set an intention—to grow, to create, to help—you're using the gift of existence.

2. Blessings Exist Because You Exist

Blessings don't just happen randomly. They flow to you because you're here to receive them.

The love from your Divine Guides, the kindness of others, the unexpected opportunities—all of it exists for you because you are here to experience it.

3. Gratitude Exists Because You Exist

You can only feel gratitude because you are here to recognize what life gives you.

When you pause and truly acknowledge the gift of simply existing, gratitude fills every part of you. And the more gratitude you feel, the more life gives you to be grateful for.

How It All Connects:

- Your existence → allows you to set intentions.

- Your intentions → help you recognize blessings.

- Your blessings → inspire gratitude.

When you truly appreciate your existence, your intentions become clearer, your blessings become visible, and gratitude becomes second nature.

Thank your existence. It is the foundation of everything you think, feel, and achieve.

Try this:

Each morning, take a moment to say:

One thing you're grateful for.

One intention for the day.

Watch how your energy shifts when you start with appreciation and purpose.

And here's something even deeper—when you truly honor your existence, you begin to trust life's flow. You stop resisting, and instead, you surrender to something bigger. That's where we're headed next: Surrender to Life.

Your Habit, Your Transformation

Imagine integrating these 12 elements into your daily life. Imagine the shift in your energy, success, and happiness.

The key is not perfection—it's consistency. Start with one. Let it become part of you. And watch how your life transforms.

But what thoughts you must keep inside your mind when you practice this habit? Let's explore The Thought Flow Behind This Habit...

5. The Process of the 12-Minute Daily Habit

Find a quiet place.

sit down,

palm open up on the thigh,

spine erect,

chin up,

shoulder relax

close your eyes

Slowly breathe in and out 3 times.

This process is silent observation. One minute each on following areas.

1. Hear Your Sound

Observe the various sounds around you—within your surroundings, your body, and your mind.

Hints: - Try to reach out to listen beyond the usual loud sounds around you. See if you can sense a sound coming from your body parts and from mind in the farthest galaxy or from the deepest core within yourself.

Tune in with your inner ears, not just your physical ones. Some people hear it as a mantra gifted by their guru, while others experience it as a universal hum—something that connects them to an infinite power. But don't worry if you don't recognize any sound yet. Just feel the humming sound.

Let the humming arise naturally—not from your mouth, not even from your conscious mind. Let it flow from the infinite, from the vastness of existence itself. Just observe the sound as it reaches you. Stay in that space—less thinking, more witnessing.

2. See Your Light

Observe the inner light shining within your mind.

Hints: - shift your focus inward and look for a light within you. It could be a soft flickering candle, a radiant diamond, the warmth of the sun, or a distant star shining inside your heart. That light is YOU—the real you. The pure consciousness that observes everything. The eternal, limitless, and powerful YOU.

Stay with this light for a moment. This isn't just imagination— it's a way to unlock deeper truths about yourself and life. Let the light rest wherever it feels natural, at your heart or between eyebrows, or any other place and keep your attention on it. If a word, phrase, or mantra resonates with you, let it blend into this moment. Just be with your inner light—no thoughts, no judgments, no expectations. Simply witness and immerse yourself in your own presence."

3. Acknowledge Your Body

Observe your body—every part, every function, and the trillions of cells within you. Acknowledge it.

Hints: - Take a deep breath in... and slowly exhale. Now, gently shift your focus to your body. This body is your instrument—your connection to the physical world. Through it, you experience life, sense emotions, and interact with everything around you.

Now, begin scanning your body from your toes to your forehead. Feel each part, even if just for a moment. Every cell in your body is alive, working in harmony to support you. Acknowledge this incredible system within you.

Now, bring a gentle smile to your face. Let that smile radiate through every part of you, spreading warmth to every cell. Just be in this experience—fully present, fully aware. Observe yourself as a witness. Your body is real, and it is yours for this moment.

4. Enjoy Your Breath

Let your breath flow naturally—no control, just observation. Feel it. Enjoy it.

Hints: - Now, bring your attention to your breath. Just like your body, your breath is real and ever-present. Simply observe it—no need to change or control it. Notice its natural rhythm, the depth of each inhale, and the ease of each exhale. Feel the soothing flow of air moving in and out, bringing relaxation and peace. Stay in this moment, enjoy it.

5. Accompany Your Mind

Observe your thoughts as they flow from one to another. Follow them with awareness.

Hints: - Now, shift your attention to your mind. Your mind is a space filled with thoughts—sometimes completely still, other times expanding infinitely. It can focus like a laser or open up like the vast sky. Just watch it without interfering.

When your mind settles into the present moment, it reveals its true nature. If it wanders, let it. Simply stay aware. Don't try to stop or control your thoughts—just observe them. Notice where your mind flows naturally, and be fully present with whatever arises.

6. Recognize Your Intellect

Observe your intellect as it receives signals to shape your destiny while also operating through free will. Recognize it.

Hints: - Now, recognize that part of your mind that interprets, analyzes, and differentiates—your intellect. It's where you exercise free will, yet it also receives signals that shape your destiny, guided by the collective intelligence, super consciousness, or universal power.

Your intellect is the bridge between your body,mind and universal power. It helps you make sense of the world, guiding your choices and perceptions. Take a moment to observe it. Simply watch how it works—without judgment, without interference. Just be aware of this powerful tool within you.

7. Realize Your Memory

Observe your memory—its vast capacity to store and retrieve data, information, and knowledge.Realize it.

Hints: Now, turn your attention to your memory—one of the most extraordinary aspects of your being. It holds everything, from the name of your best friend to the knowledge you need in critical moments.

Your memory doesn't just store information randomly; it follows the instructions of your intellect, deciding what to keep and how to retrieve it. Take a moment to appreciate its immense power. It's a vast, intelligent system working for you every single day. Simply realize of its incredible potential.

8. Observe Your Ego

Observe your ego as it arises in your body and mind. It shapes your identity and creates your unique self-image.

Hints: - Now, bring your attention to your ego—the part of you that gives you identity. It's what makes you say, "I am a good father," "I am successful," "I am beautiful." Your ego defines how you see yourself and how you differentiate from others.

Take a moment to simply observe it. No need to judge or change anything—just be aware of its presence. As you watch it, you'll naturally begin to release what no longer serves you. Stay in this awareness for a few moments, just witnessing.

9. Be Your Self

Observe your true self—beyond body and mind. Simply be.

Hints: - Now, go even deeper—beyond your body, beyond your mind. You are not just your thoughts. You are not just your physical existence. You are something far greater.

Realize this: You are a tiny yet powerful part of the universe. Nothing truly belongs to you—everything is unfolding as part of a grand design. The moment you surrender to this truth, you align with the infinite universal power.

This is the ultimate principle of life. What we call "destiny" and what we call

"free will" are simply two sides of the same coin. Just be present in this awareness.

10. Accept Your Present

Observe this moment. Let go of thoughts. Experience the real you, here and now. Accept it.

Hints: -Life has already flowed through different situations, emotions, people, and experiences. Your past unfolded exactly as it was meant to, and your future will shape itself as per the grand design of your life.

But there's only one place where life is truly happening—RIGHT NOW.

So, bring your focus to this very moment. Observe your existence—both the world around you and the world within you. The past is just a memory. The future is only an imagination. But the present? The present is real.

Feel it. Embrace it. Live it—fully, completely, right here, right now.

11. Purify Your World

Observe the world, your body, mind, and surroundings. Let your inner light dissolve negative thoughts, heal body pains, and cleanse your environment. Purify it.

Hints: - Your body, your mind, your surroundings—this is your world. Now, close your eyes and imagine a powerful light within you—a pure, universal force of healing and transformation.

Let this light dissolve any negativity, gently soothing and healing any pain in your body. Allow it to cleanse your mind, washing away worries and doubts.

Now, let this light expand beyond you, touching everything around you. Feel its warmth, its purity. Let noble thoughts flow in from all directions and purify your world.

12. Thank Your Existence

Observe your existence with intention, receive blessings with openness, and express gratitude wholeheartedly. Thank it.

Hints: - Now, take a moment to reflect on your intentions—your three main goals, your deepest aspirations. Let them surface in your awareness with clarity and purpose.

Now, open yourself to receive blessings—from Mother Earth, from your parents, ancestors, gurus, and all the divine sources that guide you. Feel their presence as expressions of the universal energy that supports and fuels your growth.

With a heart full of gratitude, acknowledge the collective intelligence, the super consciousness—the very fabric of existence that has orchestrated everything for your journey. Thank it.

What's Next?

Now that you've aligned with your existence at every level, let's explore the next big question: How This Habit Uncovers the Authentic You. Are you ready to dive deeper?

6. How This Habit Uncovers the Real You

Have you ever felt like you're constantly doing but never really being? That life keeps moving, but you rarely get a moment to truly check in with yourself? We're surrounded by distractions—work, social media, expectations—so much that we forget who we really are beneath it all.

This 12-minute habit is designed to strip away the noise and bring you back to your core. It's not about adding more to your life—it's about removing what's unnecessary so that your true self naturally shines through.

By dedicating just 12 minutes a day, you're training yourself to observe—without judgment, without trying to change anything. This simple act of observation is powerful because:

- It separates who you are from what you experience

- if strengthens your ability to stay present and aware

- It rewires your mind to operate from clarity instead of autopilot

- It helps you detach from limiting beliefs and external influences

Now, let's break down how each step works to uncover the real you.

1. Hear Your Sound – Finding Your Connection to Existence

Why it works: Sound is the most subtle yet profound connection to your presence. Tuning in to the sounds around and within you brings deep awareness.

How it transforms you: When you truly *listen*, beyond the usual noise, you may notice a hum—a universal vibration that connects you to something much larger. Over time, this trains you to be more receptive to subtle energies and intuition.

****

2. See Your Light – Discovering the Observer Within

Why it works: Light represents awareness. By turning inward and visualizing your inner light, you shift from identifying with thoughts to recognizing the *observer* behind them.

How it transforms you: The more you practice, the more you start experiencing yourself as pure awareness—not just a person with responsibilities but as a limitless presence.

****

3. Acknowledge Your Body – Understanding Your Physical Existence

Why it works: Your body is your first identity in this world. But most people either ignore it or over-identify with it. This step creates a balanced relationship with your body.

How it transforms you: By feeling every part of yourself and appreciating the trillions of living cells working in harmony, you develop gratitude and deeper self-care. You start treating your body as your most valuable asset rather than taking it for granted.

$$**********$$

4. Enjoy Your Breath – Becoming Fully Present

Why it works: Your breath is the only thing that's always in the present moment. Observing it anchors you here and now.

How it transforms you: Instead of chasing past regrets or future worries, you start finding peace in simply being. Your breath becomes your guide to calmness, focus, and balance.

$$**********$$

5. Accompany Your Mind – Breaking Free from Thought Loops

Why it works: Your mind is always active, jumping from one thought to another. Instead of controlling it, you observe it.

How it transforms you: By stepping back and watching your thoughts, you stop being trapped by them. You become the master of your mind instead of its prisoner.

$$**********$$

6. Recognize Your Intellect – Understanding How You Shape Your Reality

Why it works: Your intellect interprets everything you see, hear, and experience. But are you using it, or is it using you?

How it transforms you: Once you recognize how your intellect forms beliefs, judgments, and decisions, you can start making choices from a place of clarity instead of unconscious conditioning.

****

7. Realize Your Memory – Learning from the Past Without Being Stuck in It

Why it works: Your memory is a vast library. It shapes your identity, but it also traps you in past emotions.

How it transforms you: By consciously observing your memory instead of being controlled by it, you learn to use past experiences wisely—without letting them dictate your present or future.

****

8. Observe Your Ego – Seeing Yourself Beyond Labels

Why it works: Your ego creates your sense of "I am." But most of our suffering comes from over-identifying with roles, titles, and expectations.

How it transforms you: When you observe your ego, you start seeing the difference between who you are and who you think you are. You become more humble, open, and authentic.

****

9. Be Your Self – Experiencing the Real You Beyond Body & Mind

Why it works: Beneath your thoughts, emotions, and ego, there is something deeper. That's you.

How it transforms you: The more you sit in this awareness, the more you realize—you are not limited by your body, job, or achievements. You are something infinite, unshaken, and deeply powerful.

****

10. Accept Your Present – Embracing What Is, Right Now

Why it works: Most stress comes from resisting reality—either wishing the past were different or worrying about the future.

How it transforms you: When you accept the present as it is, you stop wasting energy fighting reality. This allows you to respond with clarity instead of reacting with fear or regret.

****

11. Purify Your World – Letting Go of Negativity

Why it works: Energy is real. Negative thoughts, tensions, and past burdens stay within you unless you consciously release them.

How it transforms you: By visualizing inner light cleansing your body, mind, and surroundings, you create a habit of renewal. This makes you naturally more peaceful, positive, and energized.

****

12. Thank Your Existence – Receiving & Expressing Gratitude

Why it works: Intentions give direction. Blessing transfer you more energy. Gratitude shifts your mindset from lacking to abundance. It aligns you with universal intelligence.

How it transforms you: When you take a moment to thank your Divine Guides, mentors, and the forces that have shaped you, you become more open to receiving blessings. Gratitude also rewires your brain for happiness and success. Your intentions become reality easily.

****

Why This Habit is So Powerful

Most self-improvement methods focus on adding something—new knowledge, new skills, new affirmations. But real growth happens when you remove what's blocking your natural wisdom, clarity, and authenticity.

This habit works because:

It's based on observation, not effort. The more you observe, the more clarity arises naturally.

It rewires your subconscious. By daily witnessing your thoughts, emotions, and ego, you break free from unconscious patterns.

It makes you unshakable. When you know your real self, external circumstances stop controlling your inner state.

What Will Happen When You Practice Daily?

You'll feel lighter—like a weight has been lifted from your mind.

You'll gain clarity—decisions will feel more natural and aligned.

You'll become more present—able to fully enjoy life instead of just going through the motions.

You'll experience deep self-acceptance—realizing that you were already complete all along.

All of this... from just 12 minutes a day.

The real you has always been there. It's just been covered by noise. This habit is your way of removing the layers and stepping into your true self.

So, are you ready to uncover the real you? Because you've been waiting all along.

7. Summary of the Chapter

Habits: The Unseen Force Shaping Your Future

Your future is not created by big, one-time actions but by small, daily habits. Every action you repeat is a step toward—or away from—the life you desire. The question is: Are your habits working for you or against you?

While destiny plays a role, your habits determine how you respond to life's opportunities. The universe presents possibilities, but only your habits decide whether you act on them.

Harnessing the Power of Intentional Habits

Most of life runs on autopilot. The key to success is shifting from passive habits (unconscious patterns) to intentional habits (ones that serve your growth).

- Neuroscience proves that repetition strengthens neural pathways. The more you repeat a habit, the more automatic it becomes.

- Intentional habits align your actions with your highest goals, reducing decision fatigue and building momentum.

- Success isn't about working harder—it's about working smarter.

Why 12 Minutes Can Transform Your Life

Most personal growth plans fail because they require too much effort. But 12 minutes is short enough to fit into any schedule while still being powerful enough to rewire your mind.

- Small, consistent actions create lasting impact.

- Focused intention during those 12 minutes builds clarity and alignment.

- It's easy to maintain, preventing burnout and resistance.

The 12 Key Elements of This Practice

This habit is not just about repetition—it's about awareness. Each minute is dedicated to one of the following elements:

1. Hear Your Sound – Tuning in to the subtle vibrations around and within you.

2. See Your Light – Recognizing the observer within.

3. Acknowledge Your Body – Honoring your physical existence.

4. Enjoy Your Breath – Anchoring yourself to the life force.

5. Accompany Your Mind – Observing thoughts without attachment.

6. Recognize Your Intellect – Understanding how you interpret reality.

7. Realize Your Memory – Use the immense potential of memory without being trapped in past learning.

8. Observe Your Ego – Seeing beyond labels and self-identifications.

9. Be Your Self – Experiencing the unshaken, limitless you.

10. Accept Your Present – Letting go of past regrets and future worries.

11. Purify Your World – Removing negativity from your body, mind, and surroundings.

12. Thank Your Existence – Receiving blessings and expressing gratitude & project your intentions

The Process of the 12-Minute Daily Habit

- Find a quiet place

- Sit with an open posture, spine erect, shoulders relaxed

- Take three deep breaths

- Observe the 12 elements for one minute each

No force. No effort. Just witnessing.

How This Habit Uncovers the Real You

By practicing daily:

- You separate who you are from what you experience.

- You strengthen your ability to stay present and aware.

- You rewire your subconscious to operate with clarity.

- You detach from limiting beliefs and external influences.

Your Habit, Your Transformation

Big changes don't happen overnight. But small, consistent shifts—just 12 minutes a day—can completely transform your life. This practice is not about adding more but about removing the layers that hide your authentic self.

Are you ready to automate your growth with one powerful habit?

Chapter 3

Authentic

1. Unveiling Your Authentic Self

My friend, let me share something powerful with you—your authentic self is the key to effortless, unstoppable growth.

Think about it. Have you ever felt like life is a constant uphill battle? Like success, happiness, and fulfillment are things you have to chase?

That's because most self-improvement advice out there forces you into rigid routines, endless to-do lists, and external motivation. It's like trying to fit into a mold that was never meant for you. But what if growth didn't have to feel like a struggle?

What if, instead of pushing yourself to "become better," you simply aligned with who you truly are?

Here's the secret: When you live as your authentic self, life flows. Success isn't something you force—it's something that naturally happens. You don't chase opportunities—they come to you. And the best part? This isn't just about one area of life. Your authenticity transforms everything.

How Authenticity Impacts Every Part of Your Life

- Health – When you respect your body and mind, self-care becomes second nature. You naturally crave movement, good food, rest, and peace—no forcing, no guilt, just effortless well-being.

- Wealth – When your work aligns with your skills and passions, money follows. You don't need to chase wealth—it finds you. Financial success becomes a byproduct of being in alignment.

- Relationships – When you're real, you attract real connections. Trust, love, and respect thrive when you show up as your true self, rather than trying to please or impress others.

- Job/Business – Work stops feeling like a grind when it matches your purpose. Creativity, success, and influence flow naturally because you're no longer fighting against yourself.

- Recreation – You stop doing things just because others say they're fun. Instead, you choose activities that genuinely refresh and energize you, making life joyful and balanced.

- Contribution – Helping others isn't a duty—it's something you want to do because it's a natural extension of who you are. And that? That's fulfillment.

- Spirituality – As you align with your true self, you experience a deeper connection with the universe, clarity, and inner peace. You stop searching outside and start feeling whole within.

This is why authenticity is everything.

The moment you stop trying to be someone else and start living as YOU, life expands in the most beautiful way.

No force. No struggle. Just effortless, automatic growth.

So, my friend, are you ready to step into your true self?

Good—because now, we're going to why it matters

Next: **Why an Authentic Personality Matters**

2. Why an Authentic Personality Matters

My friend, have you ever paused for a moment and asked yourself, "Who am I, really?"

Not your job title. Not the roles you play. Not what the world expects of you. But the real, raw, unfiltered YOU.

Somewhere beneath the layers of expectations, conditioning, and self-doubt, there exists a version of you that is pure, powerful, and authentically YOU. And here's the secret—when you start living from that place, everything shifts.

Happiness? It's no longer something you chase.

Success? It stops being a struggle and starts becoming effortless.

Freedom? It becomes your natural state, not just an idea.

But here's the problem...

Why Most People Feel Lost

In this fast-moving world, most people feel stuck, stressed, and dissatisfied. They wake up every day and follow a script written by society—do this, achieve that, be like them—but deep inside, something feels off.

They're living a life that's not truly theirs. And that disconnect? That's what creates the invisible prison of stress, frustration, and lack of clarity.

But the moment you align with your authentic self, life takes on a new meaning:

- Clarity Becomes Your Superpower – Decision-making feels natural because you no longer second-guess yourself. You just know.

- Fulfillment Comes Naturally – You stop living by society's checklist and start living by what truly feels right for you.

- You Unlock Limitless Potential – The more you embrace your real self, the more unstoppable you become.

Sounds incredible, right? So why don't more people live this way?

What's Blocking Your Authentic Self?

If your authentic self is already within you, why is it so hard to feel it?

Because it's buried under layers of:

- Ego – The mask you wear to fit in, compete, or prove yourself.

- Conditioning – Beliefs you've absorbed from family, culture, and society—many of which aren't even yours.

- Fear – The doubts that whisper, "What if I'm not enough?"

- External Expectations – The pressure to live life on someone else's terms.

But here's the truth: These layers are NOT you. They're just barriers keeping you from the life that was meant for you. And once you start peeling them away, something incredible happens...

Recognizing Your Authentic Self

Your authentic self doesn't shout. It whispers.

It's not found in the noise of the world—it's found in the quiet moments when you feel most alive.

So, how do you start reconnecting with it?

1. Look at Your Values – What truly matters to you, beyond what others expect?

2. Follow Your Joy – What activities make you feel energized and fulfilled? That's a clue.

3. Listen to Your Intuition – There's a voice within you that has always known the way. Trust it.

But recognizing your true self is just the first step. The real transformation begins when you start living as that person every single day.

Living as Your Authentic Self

Once you reconnect with your authentic self, you'll notice something: Life flows.

- You stop hiding. You accept yourself completely—flaws, strengths, and all.

- Your choices become effortless. You make decisions based on what aligns with your truth, not external pressure.

- You live in the present. You stop overthinking the past or fearing the future—you just be.

And guess what? This isn't something that takes years to figure out. Just 12 minutes a day—spent in self-reflection, awareness, and realignment—can transform everything.

The Gift of Authenticity

When you embrace your authentic self, something magical happens...

You become magnetic. The right people, opportunities, and experiences naturally come your way. You stop chasing. Instead, life unfolds for you.

Because the truth is—you don't need to become your authentic self. You already ARE. This journey isn't about adding more to yourself; it's about removing what isn't you so your true essence can shine.

And when that happens? Growth becomes automatic. Life stops feeling like a battle and starts feeling like an adventure.

But here's the big question: How do you get there?

How do you move from confusion to clarity, from struggle to flow, from limitation to expansion?

That, my friend, is exactly what we'll explore next...

3. The Path to be Authentic

My friend, let me share a secret with you—personal growth isn't about doing more.

We've been conditioned to believe that success comes from endless effort—grinding harder, working longer, stacking productivity hacks, and forcing ourselves into rigid routines. And sure, strategies help... but they don't create real transformation.

Why? Because they focus on "what you do" instead of "who you are".

The Shift: From Doing to Being

Most people spend their lives chasing success—pushing, struggling, trying to "fix" themselves with external solutions. But what if success didn't have to be chased?

What if growth could happen naturally, just by being aligned with your true self?

This is the paradigm shift—the transformation from obsessing over external actions to living from within. When you shift from doing to being, everything changes:

- From External to Internal – Instead of relying on outside tactics, you build deep inner clarity.

- From Force to Flow – Growth stops feeling like an uphill battle. It becomes effortless.

- From Complexity to Simplicity – You don't need a hundred strategies. Just 12 minutes a day of deep self-connection can unlock unstoppable transformation.

Why "Who You Are" Matters More Than "What You Do"

Think about it—your actions come from your inner state.

If you're feeling stressed, confused, or disconnected, no strategy in the world will work for you. But when you're clear, aligned, and intentional, the right actions happen effortlessly.

Let's break it down:

- A person who is courageous doesn't need a strategy to overcome fear—they just take bold action.

- A person who is consistent doesn't need complicated time-management tools—they simply follow through.

- A person who is clear doesn't need endless decision-making frameworks—they just know the right path.

When you focus on being, growth happens automatically. You don't have to force it—it emerges naturally.

The Power of Authentic Alignment

At the core of this shift is authentic alignment—living in harmony with your values, purpose, and unique strengths. When you are aligned:

- Your actions naturally support your goals.

- You feel energized and inspired, not drained and overwhelmed.

- You build habits that last—because they don't feel forced.

This is the foundation of TRUE Growth. No cookie-cutter formulas. No borrowed blueprints. Just YOU stepping into your full power.

How to Automate Your Growth

Ready to shift? Here's how you can start:

1. Focus on Inner Transformation – Instead of chasing external tactics, spend time understanding yourself—your values, strengths, and purpose.

2. Adopt Small, Intentional Habits – You don't need to overhaul your life. Just 12 minutes a day spent in reflection, mindfulness, or journaling can create massive change.

3. Let Growth Emerge Naturally – Stop forcing progress. When your inner world is right, the right actions will follow effortlessly.

4. Measure Success by Your State of Being – Instead of only tracking external results, ask yourself: Am I more joyful? More present? More aligned with my purpose? These are the real signs of transformation.

A Life of Effortless Growth

This isn't just a new approach—it's a complete redefinition of success.

When you stop trying to "fix" yourself with external strategies and start being your true self:

- Growth becomes automated.

- Success feels natural and fulfilling

- You experience deeper happiness, freedom, and prosperity.

This is what "Automate Your Growth" is all about.

You don't need more strategies.

You just need to BE who you were always meant to be.

And that leads us to the ultimate truth—The Power of Being Over Doing. Let's explore this together...

4. The Power of Being Over Doing

My friend, let me share something that might completely shift the way you see success, growth, and even life itself.

Most of us have been taught that success comes from doing more—working harder, checking off to-do lists, grinding through strategies, and pushing ourselves constantly. And yes, action is important. But what if I told you that real, effortless, unstoppable success doesn't come from doing more?

It comes from being more.

The Hidden Truth About Effortless Success

Think about the people who inspire you the most—the ones who seem to achieve greatness with ease. Are they just following a set of strategies? No.

They embody certain qualities. They are courageous, clear, and consistent. Their success isn't about what they do—it's about who they are.

That's the difference between doing and being.

Why Being is More Powerful Than Doing

1. Doing is Limited. Being is Infinite.

Actions are always tied to specific situations. But who you are shapes everything you do. A person who is courageous doesn't need a special strategy to take bold steps—they just act. A person who is confident doesn't need motivation to show up—they just do.

But if you operate from fear, doubt, or confusion, no amount of external strategy will ever feel like enough.

2. Being Creates Authenticity.

When you focus only on doing, you feel pressure—to perform, to conform, to meet expectations. It's exhausting.

But when you focus on being, you align with your true nature. You don't act because you have to—you act because it feels natural. No more forcing. No more pretending. Just pure authenticity.

3. Being Drives Sustainable Growth.

Doing often feels like an uphill battle, requiring constant effort. But when you are aligned—with clarity, courage, and purpose—growth becomes effortless. You don't have to force change. It simply emerges from within you.

4. Being Influences Others Instantly.

Your state of being is contagious. People can sense authenticity, confidence, and purpose. You don't need to prove yourself—they just feel it.

When you embody clarity, courage, and joy, you naturally inspire and lead—without even trying.

The Shift from Doing to Being

So the key question isn't:

"What should I do?"

Instead, ask yourself:

"Who should I become?"

When you shift your focus to qualities like clarity, consistency, and courage, your actions will take care of themselves. You won't need to struggle to stay disciplined. The right habits will form automatically.

And guess what?

This isn't hard. It doesn't take years of struggle.

With a simple 12-minute daily practice, you can:

- Develop deep self-awareness and discover your authentic self.

- Let go of unnecessary struggle and resistance.

- Create a natural flow where success comes easily.

Because being doesn't mean doing nothing—it means doing the right things effortlessly.

Becoming an Authentic Personality: The Secret to Limitless Freedom

Let's go deeper.

True power comes from authenticity—being fully, unapologetically YOU.

But let's be honest—most people aren't living their true lives. They're trapped in expectations, self-doubt, and resistance. They're trying to fit in instead of standing out.

Authenticity is about breaking free. It's about aligning with your deepest values, embracing your uniqueness, and living with unstoppable confidence.

What It Means to Be Authentic

1. Self-Awareness – Knowing your strengths, purpose, and passions.

2. Honesty – Being real with yourself and others, no matter how uncomfortable.

3. Alignment – Making sure your actions match your inner truth.

4. Fearlessness – Letting go of the need for approval.

Why Authenticity Unlocks Everything

You'll feel a deep sense of peace and confidence.

Your relationships will be more meaningful and fulfilling.

You'll unlock your highest potential, contributing to the world in a unique way.

Releasing Resistance: How to Let Go and Step into Flow

Most people are fighting themselves—overthinking, doubting, and procrastinating.

This is resistance. The invisible wall stopping you from the life you truly want.

How to Break Free:

1. Recognize Resistance – Notice when you feel self-doubt, hesitation, or fear.

2. Accept & Release – Don't fight it. Acknowledge it, and let it go.

3. Replace with Power – Use gratitude, affirmations, and self-belief to shift your mindset.

4. Take Inspired Action – Act from a place of alignment, not fear.

The moment you release resistance, life begins to flow.

- Decisions become easier.

- Creativity skyrockets.

- Joy becomes your natural state.

And that's when you realize—you never had to force success. It was waiting for you all along.

The Superconscious State: Living Beyond Limits

There's a level beyond the mind—a state of clarity, intuition, and infinite potential.

This is the superconscious state—where your highest self guides your actions effortlessly.

How to Access It

1. Be Present – Stop worrying about the past or future. Live now.

2. Trust Your Intuition – Your gut knows what's right. Follow it.

3. Practice Gratitude – Gratitude shifts your energy instantly.

4. Meditate Daily – Even a few minutes will unlock deep awareness.

The Benefits of Superconscious Living

- You feel limitless joy and purpose in everything you do.

- Challenges don't overwhelm you—you handle them with ease.

- Success becomes automatic—you attract opportunities effortlessly.

The world doesn't change. You change. And when you change, everything around you shifts.

The Truth About Growth: It's Not About Doing More—It's About Becoming More

My friend, you don't need more strategies or hacks.

You don't need to push harder.

You just need to step into who you really are.

When you focus on being rather than doing...

- Growth becomes automatic.

- Success feels effortless.

- You experience true happiness, freedom, and fulfillment.

This is the power of authenticity. This is the secret to unstoppable transformation.

So the question isn't: "What should I do next?"

The real question is:

"Who am I becoming?"

And once you shift your focus to being...

Everything you desire will flow to you effortlessly.

Now that we understand why being is more powerful than doing, let's explore something even deeper—the foundation of your being.

Your VALUES.

Because your values shape who you are, and when you live in alignment with them, you unlock a life of true freedom, power, and success.

5. Summary of the Chapter

Unveiling Your Authentic Self

Most people spend their lives chasing success, happiness, and fulfillment—thinking they must do more to achieve them. But the truth is, real growth happens when you simply align with your authentic self.

When you live authentically:

- Health – Self-care becomes effortless.

- Wealth – Financial success follows passion and alignment.

- Relationships – Trust and deep connections form naturally.

- Job/Business – Work becomes fulfilling instead of a struggle.

- Recreation – Joy comes from doing what truly energizes you.

- Contribution – Helping others feels natural, not forced.

- Spirituality – You experience deep inner peace and connection

The moment you stop trying to be someone else and start living as YOU, life flows effortlessly.

Why an Authentic Personality Matters

Have you ever asked yourself, "Who am I, really?" Beyond titles, roles, and expectations? Your authentic self is buried under layers of:

- Ego – The mask you wear to fit in.

- Conditioning – Beliefs inherited from society.

- Fear – Doubts that tell you you're not enough.

  External Expectations – The pressure to conform.

  When you remove these layers:

- Clarity becomes your superpower.

- Fulfillment replaces struggle.

- You unlock limitless potential.

Authenticity isn't about becoming someone—it's about removing what isn't you.

The Path to Being Authentic

Most people focus on doing more, thinking that's the key to success. But real transformation comes from being more—shifting from:

External to Internal – Clarity comes from within, not from tactics.

Force to Flow – Growth becomes effortless.

Complexity to Simplicity – Small, intentional habits lead to massive change.

A 12-minute daily practice of self-awareness and alignment can automate personal growth without struggle.

The Power of Being Over Doing

Most people believe success comes from doing more—hustling harder, checking off to-do lists, and pushing themselves. But true success comes from who you are, not just what you do.

- Doing is limited. Being is infinite.

- Being creates authenticity. No more forcing or pretending.

- Being drives sustainable growth. Success flows effortlessly when you're aligned.

- Being influences others. Authenticity is magnetic—it naturally attracts people and opportunities.

Instead of asking, "What should I do?", ask "Who should I become?" When you embody qualities like clarity, courage, and consistency, the right actions happen automatically.

Living Beyond Limits: The Superconscious State

When you shift from overthinking and resistance to trusting your intuition and living in the present, you enter a superconscious state—a life of clarity, ease, and effortless success.

How to access it:

- Be present. Stop worrying about the past or future.

- Trust your intuition. Your gut already knows.

- Practice gratitude. It shifts your energy instantly.

- Meditate daily. Even a few minutes unlock deep awareness.

The Truth About Growth

You don't need more strategies.

You don't need to force success.

You just need to step into who you truly are.

- When you focus on being, growth becomes automatic.

- Success feels effortless.

- You experience true happiness, freedom, and fulfillment.

The real question isn't: "What should I do next?"

It's: "Who am I becoming?"

And once you shift your focus to being... everything you desire will flow effortlessly.

Chapter 4

Values

1. Six Core Values of Unstoppable Success

Hello friend, have you ever wondered why some people just seem to command respect effortlessly, while others struggle to make an impact? It all comes down to one thing—values.

Your values are not just some fancy words you put on a vision board; they are the essence of who you are. They shape your ego, guide your behavior, and define your character. And guess what? Over time, this becomes the foundation of your growth.

Think of values like the operating system of your life. The way you respond to situations, the way you treat people, the decisions you make—all of it is a reflection of your values. If honesty is a core value, you will naturally speak the truth, even when it's uncomfortable. If discipline is a value, you won't need external motivation to stay consistent in your work.

Your Values, Your Identity

Ever noticed how people are remembered for their values rather than their achievements? When someone says "He's a man of integrity" or "She's incredibly compassionate," that's their true identity.

Let me give you a real-life example. Imagine two engineers in the same company. One always takes shortcuts, avoids responsibility, and prioritizes personal gain. The other is reliable, works with sincerity, and helps his colleagues whenever needed. Now tell me, who do you think will be respected, trusted, and eventually grow in their career?

Your values define how people see you, and more importantly, how you see yourself.

The Growth Formula

Here's a simple truth:

- Your values shape your thoughts.

- Your thoughts influence your actions.

- Your actions build your character.

- Your character determines your growth.

If you ever feel stuck in life, ask yourself—are my values aligned with the person I want to become? Growth isn't just about learning new skills; it's about refining the foundation on which everything else is built.

Life Lesson:

If you focus on strengthening your values, success will chase you. But if you compromise on values for short-term gains, you might move fast, but you'll never feel fulfilled.

So, take a moment today and reflect—what are the top three values that define you? Are they strong enough to support the life you want to build?

Your Core Values: The Unshakable Foundation of Growth

Hey friend, let me ask you something—what truly defines a person? Is it their skills? Their wealth? Their achievements? Nope. It's their values.

Your values are the invisible force shaping your thoughts, decisions, and actions every single day. If your values are weak, life feels uncertain, scattered, and unpredictable. But when your values are strong, life becomes clear, stable, and purposeful.

So, what are those core values that truly define you? If you want real, unstoppable growth, these six values will build your foundation:

1. Courage – The Power to Face Anything

Ever felt stuck because of fear? Fear of failure, rejection, or uncertainty? Courage is what helps you move forward despite fear. It's what makes you take risks, speak your truth, and step outside your comfort zone.

Life Lesson: Every big transformation starts with a courageous decision. The moment you stop running from fear and start facing it, your life changes.

2. Clarity – The Vision That Guides You

You can have all the talent in the world, but if you don't know where you're going, you'll just wander. Clarity gives you direction. It helps you separate what truly matters from distractions.

Life Lesson: Without clarity, you waste time and energy on things that don't align with your purpose. When you have clarity, every step you take moves you closer to your dream.

3. Consistency – The Key to Mastery

Let's be honest—most people don't struggle because they lack skills. They struggle because they start something and give up too soon. Consistency is what separates those who succeed from those who almost succeed.

Life Lesson: Success isn't about doing one big thing right; it's about doing the right things repeatedly. Small, daily actions build massive results over time.

4. Capacity – The Strength to Keep Growing

Growth isn't about reaching a destination; it's about continuously expanding your abilities. Your capacity determines how much you can handle and how far you can go. The more you develop yourself—mentally, physically, and emotionally—the more you can achieve.

Life Lesson: If you want a bigger life, you need to increase your capacity. A weak foundation can't support a tall building. Likewise, without expanding your knowledge, mindset, and resilience, you'll struggle to grow.

5. Consciousness – The Awareness That Elevates You

Are you truly aware of your thoughts, emotions, and actions? Or are you just reacting to life on autopilot? Consciousness is the ability to observe yourself, understand your patterns, and make intentional choices.

Life Lesson: Most people live unconsciously, repeating the same mistakes. But when you become aware, you gain control over your life. Awareness creates transformation.

6. Caring – The Heart of True Success

At the end of the day, success means nothing if it's not built on care and kindness. Whether it's in your work, relationships, or contributions to society, genuine care makes you a person others respect and trust.

Life Lesson: People may forget your words, but they will never forget how you made them feel. The more you care, the more meaningful your success becomes.

How Strong Are Your Values?

Look at your life right now. Are these six values deeply embedded in your daily actions? Or are they just ideas that you admire but don't fully practice?

If your values are strong, your growth will be automatic—because they will shape every choice you make. But if they are weak, life will feel like an uphill battle.

The secret to unstoppable success? Strengthen your values, and success will follow.

Integrating the 6 C's into Your Life

To embody these qualities, start small. Focus on one "C" at a time, practicing it intentionally in your daily life. Over time, these principles will become second nature, shaping your character and actions effortlessly.

The Result: Personal Excellence

When you integrate courage, clarity, consistency, capacity, consciousness, and contribution into your life, you align with your highest potential. This code of honor becomes the foundation for unstoppable growth and authentic living.

Let the 6 C's guide your journey toward happiness, freedom, and prosperity. They are not just principles; they are the essence of who you are becoming.

2. How These Values Drive Your Growth?

Courage

Let's get real for a moment—are you truly happy with yourself? Are you doing what you really want to do? Are you happy with your studies, your work, your life? If not, what's stopping you?

Most of the time, it's fear. Fear of failing, fear of judgment, fear of not being good enough, fear of lacking resources, fear of not finishing what you start. But where does this fear come from? Is it something people told you? A past experience? Or is it just your mind over-processing things?

Here's the truth: Fear doesn't come from outside. It's not even from within you—it's just a reaction to uncertainty. And guess what? You can override it. The only thing faster than fear is faith— faith in yourself, faith in others, or faith in a higher power.

Faith beats fear. Always.

But how do you build faith?

- If you want faith in yourself, cultivate self-confidence (Shraddha).

- If you want faith in others, build meaningful relationships.

- If you want faith in a higher power, develop your spiritual connection.

Fear is normal—it happens to everyone. But what separates successful people is acting in spite of fear. That's courage. And that's the secret to success.

Action Points:

1. Write down 10 fears that are holding you back.

2. Identify what would happen if those fears came true.

3. List actions you can take to reduce those fears.

4. If you can't prevent a bad outcome, how will you handle it?

5. How will you accept and move forward if things don't go as planned?

****

Clarity

Now that you have courage, the next big question is—where are you going? What actions do you need to take?

You might have many goals, but if they're not clear, they're just wishes. Clarity helps you see challenges ahead so you can prepare for them. Without it, distractions will pull you in every direction.

Your goals should be S.M.A.R.T.—Specific, Measurable, Achievable, Relevant, and Time-bound. But even more important, your goals should be emotionally connected to your purpose—why they matter, how they benefit you, and who they impact.

Action Points:

1. Write down your immediate goal (to achieve within a year).

2. List your short-term goals (1-5 years).

3.   Define your long-term goals (within 15 years).

4.   Identify your ultimate life goals.

5.   Map out the destination, path, obstacles, tools, and skills you need.

6.   Find out who can help—mentors, coaches, or yourself.

****

Consistency

Clarity gives direction, but consistency is what keeps you moving. You can't just set goals and hope they happen—you need daily action.

Consistency is about building habits, tracking progress, and improving little by little—delta increments. The key is to start, even if it's imperfect. No one is perfect, and waiting for perfection only leads to procrastination.

Action Points:

1.   List the things you do consistently.

2.   List the things you want to do consistently but haven't started (e.g., exercise, meditation, learning, improving relationships).

3.   Commit to small daily actions.

4. Track your progress, analyze, and improve.

****

Capacity

Your success depends on four things: your mind, your skills, your tools, and your actions.

Capacity is your ability to learn, innovate, and adapt. Technology changes fast, and so should you. But it's not just technical skills—soft skills, leadership, and moral values are equally important.

Your thoughts create actions, and your actions create results. So, train your mind to generate positive thoughts and stay in a growth mindset.

Action Points:

1. Identify your current skills and strengths.

2. Identify the areas where you need improvement.

3. Align your learning with your goals.

4. Learn, apply, and teach what you learn.

5. Use tools and technology to work smarter, not harder.

****

Consciousness

For sustainable success, you need awareness. Awareness of your actions, their impact, and your responsibilities to yourself and society.

High consciousness helps you respond instead of reacting. It keeps you from making impulsive mistakes, whether in relationships, career, or money. It helps you see ahead and make better decisions.

There are different stages of action:

- Unconsciously Incompetent (Don't know what you don't know)

- Consciously Incompetent (Know what you don't know but haven't acted)

- Consciously Competent (Practicing, improving)

- Unconsciously Competent (Mastery—things become second nature)

Success isn't just about you—it's about how your success impacts others. Be ethical, responsible, and mindful.

Action Points:

1. Be aware of how your words, thoughts, and actions impact others.

2. Strive for transparency and ethical decision-making.

3. Improve your awareness through mindfulness and self-reflection.

****

Caring

The highest level of personal growth is serving others. The more you give—whether it's time, money, knowledge, or support—the more you grow.

When you focus on serving rather than just achieving, stress disappears. You act from a place of abundance rather than fear. Givers always win in the long run.

Action Points:

1. Find ways to serve others—mentoring, sharing knowledge, volunteering.

2. Give without expecting immediate returns.

3. Build a mindset of contribution, not just consumption.

Final Thought:

Courage and Clarity shape your thoughts.

Consistency and Capacity drive your actions.

Consciousness and Caring define your impact.

When you master these, personal growth isn't just something you do—it becomes a way of life.

3. Values in Decision-Making and Leadership

Let's talk about something that influences every single decision we make—our values. Whether we realize it or not, our values act like an internal GPS, guiding us toward the right choices in life and work.

When our values are clear, our decisions become simpler. There's no second-guessing, no confusion—just clarity and confidence.

How Values Shape Everyday Decisions in Personal and Professional Life

Imagine you're leading a project at work. The deadline is tight, and a shortcut could save you time—but it means compromising on quality. Now, if integrity is one of your core values, you won't even consider cutting corners. You'll find a way to deliver both quality and efficiency. On the other hand, if your primary value is quick success at any cost, you might justify the shortcut. See how your values dictate the path you take?

This applies to every part of life.

- If you value health, you'll make time for exercise, even on a busy day.

- If you value family, you won't ignore your loved ones just because work gets hectic.

- If you value growth, you'll invest in learning instead of wasting time on distractions.

Every choice—big or small—is filtered through the lens of what we truly value.

The Connection Between Strong Values and Authentic Leadership

Now, let's connect this to leadership. The best leaders don't just talk about values—they live them. That's what makes them authentic. People trust and follow leaders who stay true to their principles, especially in tough times.

Authentic leaders:

- Lead with integrity, even when it's inconvenient.

- Show courage, making decisions that may not be popular but are right.

- Demonstrate consistency, aligning actions with their beliefs.

Think about an engineering leader you admire. Chances are, they built their reputation not just on technical skills but on unshakable values.

Every decision we make—whether personal or professional—is shaped by our values. The stronger and clearer our values are, the easier it becomes to make decisions without hesitation or doubt. When values are weak or unclear, we struggle with choices, second-guess ourselves, and often end up in situations that don't feel right.

Authentic leadership is built on this foundation. Great leaders don't just talk about values—they live them in their decisions, actions, and influence. The six core values of unstoppable success—Courage, Clarity, Consistency, Capacity, Consciousness, and Caring—serve as a powerful framework for making aligned decisions and leading with authenticity.

How Values Shape Everyday Decisions in Personal and Professional Life

Every decision, big or small, runs through an internal filter—our values. If we are clear on these six values, decision-making becomes effortless and empowering.

1. Courage – Making the Right Choice, Even When It's Hard

Many decisions require us to step out of our comfort zone—standing up for what's right, taking risks, or facing uncertainty. Without courage, we might choose the easy way out, even if it conflicts with what we truly believe in. Courage ensures we stay true to our values, even under pressure.

Ask yourself: Am I making this decision based on what's right, or am I avoiding discomfort?

2. Clarity – Removing Confusion from Decision-Making

Clarity eliminates hesitation. When we have a clear understanding of what we want and what we stand for, decisions become straightforward. Without clarity, we get stuck in overthinking and indecision, leading to stress and wasted time.

Ask yourself: Do I fully understand what I want, or am I making this decision out of confusion?

3. Consistency – Aligning Actions with Core Values

One decision aligned with your values isn't enough—you need to repeat it consistently. Leadership isn't about one-time good choices; it's about continuously making decisions that reflect integrity, honesty, and commitment. Inconsistency erodes trust, both in yourself and in others.

Ask yourself: Am I making this decision in line with my past commitments and beliefs?

4. Capacity – Strengthening Yourself to Make Better Decisions

Sometimes, we hesitate to make the right choice because we feel unprepared. Do I have the knowledge, skills, or strength to make this decision? The more we build our capacity—through learning, experience, and resilience—the more confidently we make decisions.

Ask yourself: Do I have the ability to handle the consequences of this decision? If not, what do I need to develop?

5. Consciousness – Staying Aware of the Impact of Our Decisions

A conscious leader is always aware of how decisions affect not just themselves but also their team, family, and society. Mindless decisions lead to regret, but conscious decision-making creates long-term success and fulfillment.

Ask yourself: Have I fully considered the impact of this decision on myself and others?

6. Caring – Making Decisions That Uplift Others

Leadership isn't just about personal gain; it's about caring for the bigger picture. When we make decisions with genuine concern for people—our team, clients, community—we build trust and influence. True success is measured not just by what we achieve, but by how we uplift others.

Ask yourself: Is this decision driven by selfish gain, or does it also contribute positively to others?

The Connection Between Strong Values and Authentic Leadership

The best leaders don't demand respect—they earn it through their actions. People trust and follow those who are courageous, clear, consistent, capable, conscious, and caring. These qualities set apart a true leader from just a boss.

- Leaders with courage make tough decisions, even in uncertainty.

- Leaders with clarity remove confusion and provide direction.

- Leaders with consistency earn trust by standing by their principles.

- Leaders with capacity handle challenges with strength and skill.

- Leaders with consciousness are aware of their impact and take responsibility.

- Leaders with caring create a positive, meaningful influence on others.

A leader who embodies these values doesn't just succeed in their career—they inspire others to grow, contribute, and thrive.

Final Thought

Your values define your decisions, and your decisions define your leadership. If you want to grow into a truly authentic and impactful leader, it starts with aligning your choices with the six core values.

So, ask yourself:

- Am I making decisions based on my values, or am I compromising for convenience?

- Am I leading in a way that reflects the person I want to be?

When you live by your values, leadership is not something you do—it's something you become.

4. Aligning Values with Life and Career Goals

You know what's crazy? Most people chase success without ever stopping to ask what truly matters to them. They set goals based on what society expects what their peers are doing, or what looks impressive on paper. But here's the thing—if your goals don't align with your core values, no matter how much you achieve, you'll always feel something is missing.

Let's break this down.

The Importance of Identifying and Prioritizing Personal Values

Think of values as the foundation of a house. If the foundation is weak or built on something that doesn't suit the structure, the whole thing will crumble. The same applies to life and career. If your goals aren't built on the right values, you'll always feel restless, unfulfilled, or stuck.

So, first things first—you need to know your values. Ask yourself:

- What truly matters to me?

- What are the principles I refuse to compromise on?

- What kind of person do I want to become?

Once you have clarity on your values, prioritize them. Some might be non-negotiable, while others could be flexible based on life's phases. But if you don't define them, the world will define them for you.

How Misalignment Between Values and Goals Leads to Frustration and Stagnation

Let's say you value freedom—the ability to make your own choices, control your time, and live on your own terms. But your career goal pushes you into a rigid corporate structure where you're expected to follow orders without questioning. What happens? You feel suffocated. Even if you're earning well, you feel stuck.

Or maybe you value impact—making a meaningful difference in people's lives. But your job is purely transactional, focused only on profits. Eventually, no matter how many promotions you get, you'll feel disconnected from your work.

This kind of misalignment is one of the biggest reasons people feel drained, lost, or dissatisfied even when they seem successful from the outside. They're chasing goals that don't match their soul. And when that happens, frustration, stagnation, and burnout are inevitable.

Practical Strategies to Align Values with Career Aspirations and Personal Growth

Now that we know how important value alignment is, let's get practical. We've already defined the six core values of unstoppable success—Courage, Clarity, Consistency, Capacity, Consciousness, and Caring. Let's use them as our guide to ensure our goals and daily actions stay aligned with what truly matters.

1. Courage – Make Bold Choices That Honor Your Values

If your career or life path isn't aligned with your values, it takes courage to make a change. This could mean standing up for what you believe in at work, shifting to a more fulfilling role, or even starting something of your own. Don't let fear keep you stuck in a situation that drains you.

Ask yourself: Am I making decisions that align with my true self, or am I choosing comfort over growth?

2. Clarity – Define Your Goals with Precision

Without clarity, it's easy to drift in directions that don't serve you. Take time to clearly define what success looks like for you, not based on societal expectations. Your goals should be crystal clear and deeply connected to your values.

Ask yourself: Are my goals aligned with what I genuinely care about, or am I chasing something just because it looks good?

3. Consistency – Align Daily Actions with Long-Term Vision

It's not enough to define your values once; you have to live them daily. Small, consistent actions build habits that reinforce alignment. Whether it's setting boundaries, choosing integrity over shortcuts, or prioritizing learning, consistency is the bridge between values and success.

Ask yourself: Are my daily habits reinforcing my values, or am I contradicting them in small ways?

4. Capacity – Build Skills and Strength to Stay on the Right Path

Sometimes, we know what we want, but we lack the skills or mental strength to pursue it. Expanding your capacity—whether through learning, resilience, or networking—ensures that you have the ability to stay aligned with your values even when challenges arise.

Ask yourself: Am I equipping myself with the knowledge, skills, and mindset to stay true to my path?

5. Consciousness – Stay Aware of When You're Off-Track

Misalignment doesn't happen overnight—it's often gradual. Staying conscious of your choices, behaviors, and environment ensures you catch misalignment early. Regular self-reflection, journaling, or even talking to mentors can help maintain awareness.

Ask yourself: Am I regularly checking in with myself to ensure my actions reflect my core values?

6. Caring – Align Success with Contribution

True success isn't just about personal gains; it's about how you impact others. When your career and goals align with a sense of contribution—whether to your team, family, or society—you feel a deeper sense of fulfillment.

Ask yourself: Am I considering how my success benefits others, or is it purely self-focused?

Final Thought

Aligning your values with your career and life goals isn't about making one big decision—it's about daily choices, consistent action, and conscious awareness. When you integrate courage, clarity, consistency, capacity, consciousness, and caring into your decisions, you don't just succeed—you thrive with purpose.

So, take a moment and reflect: Which of these six values am I living fully, and which one needs more attention? The answer will guide you to your next step.

5. Summary of the Chapter

Your values are the foundation of your identity. They shape your thoughts, decisions, and actions, ultimately defining your success and fulfillment. Without strong values, life feels scattered, uncertain, and reactive. But when your values are clear and deeply rooted, you gain clarity, confidence, and consistency, making success a natural byproduct.

This chapter explores six core values that create unstoppable success and how to align them with your life and career goals.

The Six Core Values of Unstoppable Success

1. Courage – The Power to Face Anything

Fear holds most people back—fear of failure, judgment, or uncertainty. Courage is the ability to act despite fear, to step outside your comfort zone, and to make bold decisions.

Key Insight: Growth begins the moment you stop running from fear and start confronting it.

Action Step: Identify one fear that's limiting you and take a small step to face it today.

****

2. Clarity – The Vision That Guides You

Without clarity, you'll feel lost, constantly second-guessing your choices. Clarity gives you direction and focus, ensuring every action moves you toward your goals.

Key Insight: The clearer your vision, the faster your progress.

Action Step: Define your top three personal and career goals and write down why they matter.

****

3. Consistency – The Key to Mastery

Many people start strong but struggle to follow through. Success isn't about intensity; it's about small, daily actions that compound over time.

Key Insight: Discipline beats motivation. Show up daily, even when you don't feel like it.

Action Step: Pick one habit aligned with your goals and commit to practicing it daily for 30 days.

****

4. Capacity – The Strength to Keep Growing

Your success is limited by what you can handle. Expanding your knowledge, mindset, and resilience increases your ability to adapt, learn, and grow.

Key Insight: A weak foundation can't support a tall building. Expand your capacity to achieve more.

Action Step: Identify one skill you need to develop and start learning it today.

****

5.Consciousness – The Awareness That Elevates You

Most people live reactively, unaware of how their thoughts and behaviors shape their outcomes. Consciousness allows you to observe your patterns, make intentional choices, and align with your purpose.

Key Insight: Awareness is the first step to real transformation.

Action Step: Start a daily reflection habit—write down one key lesson you learned each day.

****

6. Caring – The Heart of True Success

True success is not just about personal gain—it's about impact. Whether in work, relationships, or contributions to society, genuine care builds trust, respect, and long-term fulfillment.

Key Insight: People may forget your words, but they will never forget how you made them feel.

Action Step: Find one way to help someone daily—without expecting anything in return.

How These Values Drive Your Growth

Your values influence every part of your life:

- Courage helps you make bold decisions and overcome limitations.

- Clarity ensures you're moving in the right direction.

- Consistency creates habits that turn small efforts into big results.

- Capacity strengthens your ability to handle challenges and keep evolving.

- Consciousness helps you stay aware, make better choices, and avoid distractions.

- Caring builds strong relationships, meaningful success, and lasting impact.

When your values are strong and aligned, success follows effortlessly.

The Role of Values in Decision-Making and Leadership

Your values act as an internal GPS, guiding every decision—whether in personal life or leadership. When your values are clear, decisions become easier.

- If integrity is a value, you'll never consider taking shortcuts.

- If health is a value, you'll prioritize exercise and self-care.

- If growth is a value, you'll invest in learning instead of wasting time on distractions.

The best leaders don't just talk about values—they live them. This builds trust, influence, and authenticity, setting them apart from ordinary managers.

Action Step: Think of a recent decision—did it align with your values? If not, what needs to change?

Aligning Your Values with Your Life and Career Goals

Most people chase success based on societal expectations rather than what truly fulfills them. If your goals don't align with your values, you'll always feel something is missing.

Why Alignment Matters: A career that contradicts your values leads to frustration, burnout, and dissatisfaction. True success happens when your work aligns with who you are.

How to Align Values with Career Goals:

If Clarity is your value, define your vision and eliminate distractions.

If Courage is your value, take bold actions—apply for that job, start that business, or ask for that raise.

If Consistency is your value, develop daily work habits that keep you on track.

If Capacity is your value, keep learning, upskilling, and expanding your potential.

If Consciousness is your value, make purpose-driven career decisions instead of just chasing money.

If Caring is your value, find ways to serve, lead, and create impact through your work.

Action Step: Write down your top three career goals and ask yourself—do they align with your values? If not, what needs to change?

The Secret to Unstoppable Success

Your values shape your decisions, and your decisions shape your life. When you strengthen your values and align them with your goals, success becomes a natural byproduct.

- Courage and Clarity shape your thoughts.

- Consistency and Capacity drive your actions.

- Consciousness and Caring define your impact.

Master these six values, align them with your goals, and success will no longer be something you chase—it will be something you naturally attract.

CHAPTER 5

GROWTH

1. Why Growth Matters

Growth is essential because change is inevitable. If everything around us is constantly shifting—technology, markets, relationships, and even our own bodies—why resist it? Instead, we can choose to grow, ensuring that every change works in our favor. Growth isn't just about success in a career or financial gain; it's about holistic transformation—mind, body, relationships, and spirit.

True growth is about evolving with clarity and purpose, not just drifting with change. It's about becoming a better version of ourselves every day. That's why embracing growth is not just an option; it's the smartest choice we can make.

If we don't grow intentionally, we will be pushed around by change, often in directions we don't want. Growth ensures that we stay in control, evolve consciously, and create a life that aligns with our true potential. But for growth to be meaningful, it must be holistic and sustainable.

Why Choose Growth?

Change is happening all the time, whether we're ready for it or not. But here's the thing—while we can't stop change, we can choose how we respond to it. That's where growth comes in. Instead of being pushed around by life's changes, growth allows us to take control, steer our journey, and create the future we want.

Now, let's think about what happens when we don't grow. Stagnation isn't just standing still; it's actually moving backward. The world keeps evolving—new technologies, new challenges, new opportunities. If we stay the same, we start falling behind. It's like being on an escalator that's going down while we're trying to stand still. If we don't actively climb up, we're automatically moving in the wrong direction.

But when we grow, life opens up. Every new skill we learn, every mindset shift we embrace, and every challenge we overcome gives us more choices. Financial growth brings freedom. Emotional growth brings deeper relationships. Intellectual growth expands our perspective. When we grow in all areas, we start living on our own terms, instead of just reacting to whatever life throws at us.

And here's a powerful truth—growth builds resilience. The more we strengthen ourselves from within, the better we handle challenges. Life will always test us, but when we keep growing, we develop the inner strength to bounce back stronger. Just like a tree that grows deep roots can withstand any storm, a person who commits to growth can handle any setback.

So, my friend, if change is inevitable, why not choose growth? It's the only way to ensure that every change—big or small—works in our favor.

2. The Need for Sustainable Growth

Not all growth is good. Growth without direction can lead to burnout, imbalance, or even self-destruction. Imagine a fire—it provides warmth and energy when controlled, but if it spreads recklessly, it destroys everything in its path. Growth works the same way. Sustainable growth is about evolving steadily, in a way that aligns with our values, goals, and overall well-being.

Balanced Growth – Don't get caught up chasing success in just one area while ignoring the rest. What's the point of financial success if your health is failing or if your relationships are broken? True success is a balance—health, wealth, relationships, and inner peace all need attention. Think of life like a wheel—if one part is too small or too big, the ride becomes rough.

Self-Awareness – Growth isn't about chasing what the world calls "success." It's about discovering what truly matters to you. Just because society glorifies a certain career path, lifestyle, or achievement doesn't mean it's the right one for you. Know yourself. Grow in a way that fulfills you, not just in a way that looks impressive to others.

Consistency Over Intensity – We often believe that big transformations come from extreme efforts. But real, lasting change comes from small, daily actions. A 12-minute daily habit can transform your life more effectively than sporadic bursts of effort. It's like fitness—working out for 10 hours one day won't make you fit, but exercising for 30 minutes every day will. Growth should feel natural, not forced.

Long-Term Vision – Sustainable growth isn't about quick wins or overnight success. It's about building an authentic and unstoppable personality over time. Every little effort compounds. Focus on who you are becoming, not just what you are achieving. Think of a tree—it takes years to grow deep roots, but once strong, it stands tall for decades.

So, my friend, the key is to grow wisely, in a way that fuels your life rather than drains it. Growth should energize you, not exhaust you. Choose a path that aligns with your true self, move forward consistently, and trust that with time, you'll build something truly extraordinary.

3. What is Holistic Growth?

My friend, if you want a truly fulfilling life, you can't just grow in one area and ignore the rest. Imagine trying to ride a bicycle with one tire fully inflated and the other one flat. No matter how hard you pedal, the ride will be rough. Life works the same way. To move forward smoothly, you need to grow in all key areas, Holistic Growth

Health – Your Foundation for Everything

What's the point of success if you don't have the energy to enjoy it? Your body and mind are your greatest assets. Without good health, even the best opportunities feel like burdens.

Life Lesson: Imagine two engineers—one prioritizes health with regular exercise and a balanced diet, while the other neglects it, always "too busy" for self-care. A few years later, the first one is thriving with high energy, while the second struggles with stress, fatigue, and lifestyle diseases. Your body is your vehicle for life— keep it in top condition.

2. Wealth – Not Just Money, But Financial Freedom

Money isn't everything, but let's be honest—it gives you choices. Wealth is not just about earning more; it's about managing, growing, and using it wisely. Financial growth allows you to live freely, help others, and focus on things that truly matter.

Life Lesson: Some people earn a lot but still struggle, while others with moderate income build a secure, abundant life. The difference? Financial literacy. Growing your wealth means understanding money, making smart decisions, and investing in your future.

3. Relationships – The Quality of Life is the Quality of Your Connections

You could have all the success in the world, but if you don't have meaningful relationships, who will you share your joy with? The strength of your relationships—family, friends, colleagues—determines the depth of your happiness.

Life Lesson: An engineer working abroad once told me, "I have money, but I feel empty inside." Why? He had neglected his relationships. People matter. Success is sweeter when you have loved ones to celebrate with.

4. Contribution – The Joy of Giving

There's a special kind of happiness that comes from helping others. True growth isn't just about taking—it's about giving back. When you contribute to others, you create a legacy that lasts beyond your lifetime.

Life Lesson: Think of someone who made a real difference in your life. It could be a mentor, teacher, or friend. Now imagine being that person for someone else. Your impact is your true wealth.

5. Career – Mastery & Meaning in Your Work

Your career is more than just a paycheck—it's a platform to express your skills, creativity, and purpose. Growing in your career doesn't just mean promotions; it means becoming so good that opportunities chase you.

Life Lesson: A job can be a burden or a source of deep satisfaction. The difference? Growth. Keep learning, improving, and adding value, and your work will become a source of pride, not pressure.

6. Spirituality – Inner Peace & Purpose

Growth isn't just about external success; it's also about inner fulfillment. Whether through meditation, prayer, self-reflection, or learning from spiritual guides, nurturing your spirit gives you clarity and strength in life.

Life Lesson: A peaceful mind is a powerful mind. People chase happiness in external things, but true joy comes from within. Grow spiritually, and everything else falls into place.

7. Recreation – The Power of Joy & Rest

What's the point of working hard if you never take time to enjoy life? Growth also means learning to relax, recharge, and have fun. Hobbies, travel, music, and simple joys make life worth living.

Life Lesson: Success without joy is just another form of failure. Don't wait until "one day" to enjoy life. Make time for happiness now.

Balance is the Key

If you grow in all these areas—health, wealth, relationships, contribution, career, spirituality, and recreation—you will create a life that is not just successful, but deeply fulfilling.

4. Core Values: The Foundation of Growth

My friend, if you want to grow in life—truly grow, not just achieve temporary success—you need a strong foundation. And that foundation is built on your core values. These values are like the roots of a tree. If the roots are deep and strong, the tree stands tall, no matter how strong the wind blows.

I believe there are six core values that form the foundation of personal growth:

****

1. Courage – The Power to Take Action

Growth starts when you step out of your comfort zone. Courage isn't about being fearless—it's about moving forward despite fear. Every great achievement in life begins with a bold decision.

Life Lesson: I once met an engineer who wanted to switch careers but feared failure. He finally took the leap, upskilled himself, and today, he's thriving in his dream job. The lesson? Fear will always be there, but courage pushes you beyond limits.

****

2. Clarity – Knowing Where You Are Going

Imagine driving without a destination—you'd just waste fuel and time. Life works the same way. If you don't have clarity on what you truly want, you'll keep drifting without purpose.

Life Lesson: A successful career or relationship isn't about doing what others expect—it's about knowing what truly matters to you. Take time to reflect: Where do you want to go? Who do you want to become? With clarity, every step you take will have meaning.

****

3. Consistency – Small Efforts, Big Results

Growth isn't about doing something once and expecting miracles. Success is built through small, daily habits. Whether it's learning, exercising, or improving relationships, what you do consistently shapes your future.

Life Lesson: Think of fitness—working out for one day won't make a difference, but 30 minutes every day over months will transform you. The same applies to every area of life. Small efforts, done daily, create unstoppable results.

****

4. Capacity – Expanding Your Potential

You are capable of more than you believe. Growth happens when you expand your skills, knowledge, and mindset. The more you learn and stretch yourself, the bigger your capacity to achieve great things.

212

Life Lesson: I've seen engineers struggle with new technology, thinking, "This is too hard for me." But the ones who push themselves, keep learning, and adapt become industry leaders. Your capacity grows when you challenge yourself.

****

5. Consciousness – Awareness of Yourself & Your Actions

Many people live on autopilot, reacting to life instead of shaping it. Growth starts when you become fully aware of your thoughts, habits, and decisions. When you operate with consciousness, you start making intentional choices that align with your true self.

Life Lesson: Ever made a decision you later regretted? That's what happens when we act without awareness. Slow down. Observe yourself. Understand why you do what you do. When you become conscious, you take control of your life.

****

6. Caring – The Heart of True Growth

Real success isn't just about personal achievements—it's about how much you uplift others. Growth that lacks care and compassion is empty. The more you care for people, the stronger your impact becomes.

213

Life Lesson: Think of the greatest leaders—they don't just build wealth, they build people. Whether in family, work, or society, the more you give, the more meaningful your success becomes.

Build Your Growth on a Strong Foundation

If you live with courage, gain clarity, stay consistent, expand your capacity, stay conscious, and care for others, you will create a life of unstoppable success and deep fulfillment.

5. Career Growth as Part of Personal Growth

My friend, let's be honest—money matters. It's not everything, but it plays a huge role in shaping the quality of our lives. And where does money come from? Your career. That's why career growth is a vital part of your personal growth journey.

Your career is one of the most powerful pillars of your growth. —it provides the financial support that helps you grow in other areas like health, relationships, contribution, and even recreation. When your career thrives, you have more resources, more confidence, and more freedom to live life on your own terms.

1. Financial Stability = Freedom of Choice

When your career grows, so does your income. And when you have financial stability, you're not stuck in survival mode—you can invest in your health, take care of your loved ones, pursue your passions, and give back to society.

Life Lesson: I once knew an engineer who was incredibly skilled but never focused on career growth. Years later, he found himself struggling financially, unable to support his family's dreams. On the other hand, another engineer actively upskilled, took risks, and grew in his career—he later had the freedom to start his own business and create a life of abundance. The difference? One focused only on work, while the other focused on growth.

2. Career Growth Boosts Confidence & Self-Worth

The more you grow in your career—whether through promotions, skill development, or leadership—the more confident you become. Success in your work spills over into other areas of life. When you feel accomplished, you carry yourself with strength and assurance.

Life Lesson: Think about a time when you achieved something at work—maybe solved a tough problem, led a project, or got recognized for your efforts. Didn't it make you feel powerful?

That's what career growth does—it strengthens your belief in yourself.

3. A Strong Career Supports Your Relationships

Money problems are one of the biggest causes of stress in families and relationships. When you have financial stability, you can provide for your loved ones without constant worry. You can spend quality time with family instead of always chasing the next paycheck.

Life Lesson: I know people who are so stressed about finances that they barely enjoy time with their kids or partner. On the other hand, those who focus on career growth and financial planning have the freedom to travel, celebrate, and be present for their loved ones. Your career isn't just about you—it's about the people who depend on you too.

4. Your Career is a Platform for Impact

Your job isn't just a way to earn—it's a way to create value for others. Whether you're solving problems, building something, or leading a team, your work impacts people's lives. The more you grow, the bigger your ability to make a difference.

Life Lesson: Some people see work as a burden, but successful professionals see it as a mission. The best engineers, doctors, entrepreneurs, and leaders grow because they focus on solving bigger problems. The more valuable you become, the more opportunities open up for you.

5. Growth in Career = Growth in Mindset

A stagnant career often means a stagnant mind. When you challenge yourself, learn new skills, and take on bigger roles, you expand your thinking. Career growth forces you to evolve—not just in your job, but in the way you see life.

Life Lesson: The most successful people never stop learning. They take courses, read books, find mentors, and constantly improve. If you keep learning, you keep growing. If you stop, you start falling behind.

Grow Your Career, Grow Your Life

Your career isn't separate from your personal growth—it's a big part of it. When you invest in your career, you gain financial security, confidence, better relationships, and the ability to contribute more to the world.

6. How Authenticity Speeds Up Growth

My friend, have you ever noticed that some people seem to grow effortlessly? They don't struggle, they don't chase, yet success, happiness, and opportunities seem to flow naturally toward them. What's their secret? They are authentic.

Being an authentic personality means that you don't have to force growth—it happens automatically. When you are true to yourself, the right skills, relationships, and opportunities align with you naturally. You don't have to push. You just have to BE.

Let's explore how authenticity accelerates and automates your growth.

1. Authenticity Removes Resistance

Most struggles in life come from trying to be someone you're not. When you're authentic, there's no inner conflict—you move forward with clarity and ease.

Life Lesson: Imagine two engineers: One picks a career just for money and feels drained every day. The other follows his strengths and passion, enjoying his work. Who do you think grows faster? When you love what you do, growth is automatic.

The Key: Stop forcing yourself into roles that don't fit. Align your path with who you truly are, and everything becomes smoother.

2. Authentic People Attract the Right Opportunities

When you are authentic, people trust you. They sense your clarity, confidence, and originality. This makes you naturally magnetic—opportunities, collaborations, and success come to you without struggle.

Life Lesson: Think about someone you admire. Is it their skills alone that make them inspiring, or is it their authentic presence? The world doesn't just value expertise—it values realness. Be real, and the right people will find you.

The Key: Instead of trying to impress people, focus on being your genuine self. The right opportunities will follow.

3. When You Are Authentic, Growth Feels Effortless

Have you ever seen a river struggle to flow? No. It just moves naturally in the direction it's meant to go. Authenticity is the same. When you align with your true nature, growth happens on its own.

Life Lesson: Many people chase success in ways that don't suit them. They copy others, follow trends, and struggle. But those who grow effortlessly do so because they trust their own flow.

The Key: Instead of copying what others do, discover what works best for YOU. Growth will then happen automatically.

4. Authenticity Builds Confidence & Inner Power

Doubt comes when we live out of alignment with ourselves. When you are authentic, you trust yourself more, make better decisions, and radiate confidence. This accelerates your growth because you don't waste energy on self-doubt.

Life Lesson: Have you ever met someone who was so sure of themselves that they inspired you? That's the power of authenticity. When you believe in yourself, others believe in you too.

The Key: Don't seek validation. Trust your own voice, and confidence will follow.

5. How to Be Authentic & Automate Your Growth

So, how can you become an authentic personality and let growth happen automatically?

Know Yourself – Spend time understanding your strengths, values, and desires.

Express Your Truth – Say what you mean. Do what feels right. Live in alignment with your core.

Trust Your Natural Path – Stop forcing yourself into roles that don't fit. Follow what comes naturally.

Be Consistent – The more you live authentically, the more effortless your growth becomes.

The More Authentic You Are, The Easier Life Becomes

Growth doesn't have to be a struggle. When you are true to yourself, aligned with your values, and confident in your path, success becomes a byproduct of your existence.

7. Summary of the Chapter

Why Growth Matters?

Growth isn't optional—change is happening all around us, whether we like it or not. If we don't grow intentionally, we get left behind. True growth isn't just about career success or financial gains—it's about evolving in all aspects of life: mind, body, relationships, and spirit.

- Growth keeps you in control of your future.

- Growth opens up choices—financial, emotional, and intellectual.

- Growth builds resilience, making you stronger in tough times.

If change is inevitable, why not choose growth and make every change work in your favor?

The Need for Sustainable Growth

Not all growth is good—without balance, growth can lead to burnout or imbalance. Sustainable growth means evolving steadily in alignment with your values and well-being.

- Balanced Growth: Success in one area means nothing if your health or relationships suffer. Growth should be well-rounded.

- Self-Awareness: Don't chase growth just because society expects it—grow in ways that truly matter to you.

- Consistency Over Intensity: Small, daily actions bring lasting change, not one-time efforts.

- Long-Term Vision: Growth isn't about quick wins—it's about creating a strong foundation for lifelong success.

The key is to grow wisely and steadily—in a way that energizes you rather than exhausts you.

What is Holistic Growth?

To truly thrive, you must grow in all areas of life—not just one. Life is like a wheel—if one part is weak, the ride is rough.

1. Health – Your energy and well-being determine your ability to enjoy success.

2. Wealth – Financial growth gives you freedom and security.

3. Relationships – Meaningful connections bring deep fulfillment.

4. Contribution – Giving back creates a legacy that lasts.

5. Career – Work becomes more rewarding when you grow in skills and purpose.

6. Spirituality – Inner peace and clarity guide your decisions.

7. Recreation – Joy, rest, and hobbies make life truly fulfilling.

If you grow in all these areas, success isn't just an achievement—it's a way of life.

Core Values: The Foundation of Growth

Growth without strong values is like a house without a foundation. To grow authentically and sustainably, build your life on these six core values:

1. Courage – Growth begins when you step outside your comfort zone.

2. Clarity – Know your goals, direction, and purpose.

3. Consistency – Success comes from daily, repeated actions.

4. Capacity – Expand your knowledge, mindset, and abilities.

5. Consciousness – Self-awareness ensures you grow with purpose.

6. Caring – Growth that benefits others is the most meaningful.

Master these values, and growth will happen naturally.

Career Growth as Part of Personal Growth

Your career isn't separate from your personal growth—it's one of the biggest branches of your life tree.

- Financial Stability = Freedom – A thriving career gives you choices and security.

- Growth = Confidence – Success at work builds self-belief.

- Career Supports Relationships – Financial stress can strain relationships, but stability brings peace.

- Work = Impact – Your career is a platform to create value for others.

- Lifelong Learning = Lifelong Growth – Keep learning, or risk falling behind.

Career growth isn't just about money—it's about creating a life of freedom, confidence, and impact.

How Authenticity Speeds Up Growth

The fastest-growing people aren't the ones who force success—they're the ones who are authentic.

- Authenticity Removes Resistance – No more struggling to fit into the wrong roles.

- Authentic People Attract the Right Opportunities – People trust and respect realness.

- When You're Authentic, Growth Feels Effortless – You move naturally in the right direction.

- Authenticity Builds Confidence – Self-trust leads to powerful decision-making.

How to Automate Your Growth Through Authenticity:

- Know Yourself – Understand your strengths, values, and desires.

- Express Your Truth – Speak and act in alignment with who you are.

- Trust Your Natural Path – Stop forcing yourself into roles that don't fit.

- Be Consistent – The more you live authentically, the easier growth becomes.

Final Thought: Growth doesn't have to be a struggle. Be true to yourself, and success will follow naturally.

CHAPTER 6

MONEY

1. Money Comes from People

Do you ever thought about where money actually comes from?

It doesn't just appear in your bank account by magic. The only way money flows into your life is through people.

Your salary? A company pays you, and that company is run by people. Your business income? Customers pay you, and those customers are people. Even when you use banking apps, UPI, or online transactions, it's just a medium—at the end of the day, the money is coming from someone.

So, if money comes from people, what does that mean? Simple. If you want more money, you need to create more value for people, better relationship with them. The better you serve, they trust, the more you earn.

LIFE LESSONS:

- Stop chasing money—start focusing on people. If you figure out how to help more people, solve their problems, or make their lives better, money will automatically flow toward you.

- Your income is directly linked to the value you provide. The reason some people earn more is because they are solving bigger problems for more people. The more useful you are, the more money you attract.

- Your network is your net worth. Since money comes from people, the kind of people you surround yourself with matters. Connect with the right crowd, build strong relationships, and be in an environment where opportunities flow.

- Banks, apps, and wallets are just tools. Don't get fooled by the numbers on a screen. The real source of money is always people. Focus on relationships, trust, and service. That's how wealth is built.

You must know Money doesn't come from thin air—it comes from people. So, instead of asking, "How do I make more money?", ask "How can I serve more people?"

That's the real secret, friend. Get this right, and you'll never have to worry about money again!

2. Money Solves Problems That Lack of It Creates

Most of the problems we face in life are money-related. Think about it. The problems that come from not having money can hit every area of life.

Maybe it's your relationship with your spouse, family, relatives, or friends. Money issues can create stress, misunderstandings, and even distance in relationships. Or maybe it's your health—you don't have enough to pay medical bills or even afford proper nutrition.

What about maintaining the things you already own? You might have a house, a car, or some other asset, but if you can't pay for its maintenance, it becomes a burden instead of a blessing. Then there's the fun side of life—vacations, hobbies, and entertainment. You want to go on trips, play sports, or just have a good time, but the lack of money stops you.

And man, one of the worst feelings is when a family member or a friend is in an emergency, and they ask for help, but you can't support them financially because you don't have the money yourself. That hurts.

Even your peace of mind takes a hit. When money stress is constantly on your head, how can you sit calmly, focus, or even meditate or sleep? It affects your inner spirit. On top of that, career tension kicks in—stress about money impacts your efficiency, your discipline, and the way you perform at work.

So, what's the way out? Simple—your career is the only reliable source of money. Your profession, your skills, your ability to serve others—that's what brings money into your life. The more value you provide, the more you earn.

And listen, if you try shortcuts—stealing, cheating, or using unethical ways to make money—it will only come back to bite you harder. While borrowing also you should be careful.

So, focus on building yourself, growing your skills, and serving people in the right way. That's how you make money and keep your peace of mind.

3. Career and Money Go Hand in Hand

Your career and money are like two sides of the same coin. You can't separate them. If you want money, you need a solid career. If you want a good career, you need to focus on how you earn and grow financially. They go hand in hand.

Think about it—your career is the engine that drives your income. The better you perform, the more valuable you become, and the more money you attract. On the flip side, if you don't take your career seriously, your income suffers, and then all the money-related problems start creeping in.

Now, here's the real deal:

Money is the byproduct of the value you create. The more you solve problems for others, the more they are willing to pay you. So, instead of chasing money directly, focus on how you can serve better.

Your career growth determines your financial growth. If you stay in the same place, doing the same things without upgrading your skills, don't expect your income to grow. You need to keep learning, improving, and adapting.

Stability and security come from career mastery. When you master your profession, money flows consistently. You won't have to worry about job loss or market changes because you'll always be in demand.

Money fuels your dreams. Whether it's travel, a better lifestyle, helping your family, or even contributing to society, money gives you the freedom to do it. But that money comes from your career.

Your career isn't just about earning a salary—it's your tool for financial success, peace of mind, and a fulfilling life. Work on your career, and money will follow. Ignore your career, and you'll struggle financially.

4. The Formula for Making and Growing Money

Making money isn't just about working hard—it's a process. A step-by-step journey where you first find your expertise, develop it, let the world know about it, and then monetize it. Whether it's a job or business, the money-making formula is the same.

Step 1: Find and Develop Your Expertise

Money comes from people, right? And people pay for solutions. So, the first step is to figure out what problem you can solve. What skills do you have? What can you be really good at?

- If you're in a job, master your field—become the go-to person.

- If you're in business, build a product or service that genuinely helps people.

But just knowing something is not enough. You have to keep learning, practicing, and improving. The more skilled you are, the more valuable you become.

Step 2: Communicate Your Expertise to the World

Now, here's where most people fail—they work hard but don't let the world know about their skills. If people don't know what you do, how will they pay you for it?

- In a job? Showcase your skills, take ownership of projects, and make sure your company sees your value.

- In business? Market yourself. Use social media, networking, and content to let people know how you can help them.

The louder you communicate your value, the more opportunities will come your way. Visibility creates wealth.

Step 3: Monetize It – Convert Value into Money

Now comes the best part—getting paid for what you do. When people recognize your expertise, they'll be willing to pay you. But you have to ask for it!

- In a job? Negotiate your salary, aim for promotions, and increase your worth to the company.

- In business? Price your services well, sell confidently, and ensure your customers see the value in paying you.

How Money Flows in Reality

You solve a problem → People see your value → They pay you for it.

That's it. It's not luck, not shortcuts, not magic. It's a process.

Life Lessons on Earning Money

- Money is an exchange of value – You don't get paid for time; you get paid for the impact you create.

- Skills alone won't make you rich – You have to communicate and sell your expertise.

- No one will pay you if they don't know you exist – Be visible, be known.

- Money follows trust – Build strong relationships, offer value, and rise your energy than people will get attracted to you ,buy, and keep coming back.

So, if you want to earn more, don't just sit and hope for money. Find your expertise, build it, tell the world about it, and confidently ask for what you're worth. Your worth is how you can help them to be better than present situation. That's the real process of wealth creation.

5. Money: The Hidden Fuel for Growth

Your career and Your professional growth earn you money. Hat money will fuel every areas of your life's growth—health, wealth, relationships, career, recreation, spirituality, and contribution.

If your job or business is only giving you money but ruining the rest of your life, you're doing it wrong.

Why Do You Make Money? To Grow in Every Area!

- Health – If you don't invest in your body, where will you live? Money helps you eat right, stay fit, and get medical care when needed. No point making crores if you're too sick to enjoy it.

- Wealth – Earning money is one thing, but growing and managing it is another. Wealth gives you security and freedom—so you don't have to work under stress forever.

- Relationships – Financial stress breaks families and friendships. But when you have stability, you can support your loved ones, take care of parents, and spend quality time with family.

- Career – Growth never stops. Whether you're in a job or business, investing in learning and skill-building ensures you stay ahead and keep earning.

- Recreation – Life isn't just about work. You need breaks, vacations, and fun to stay mentally fresh. Money gives you the freedom to enjoy these moments without guilt.

- Spirituality – Peace of mind comes when you're not constantly worrying about survival. When money problems are sorted, you can focus on deeper things—your purpose, meditation, and inner growth.

- Contribution –True success is when you can give back. Whether it's helping family, supporting a cause, or uplifting society, money allows you to make a bigger impact.

Life Lessons About Money & Growth

- Money is a tool, not the goal. Use it to build a complete life.

- Balance is everything. If career growth comes at the cost of health or relationships, that's not real success.

- Grow in every area. If you're only focused on making money and ignoring the rest, you'll feel empty in the long run.

- Success is about freedom. The goal is to reach a stage where money works for you, not the other way around.

So, you don't just chase money—use your professional growth to create a life where every area is thriving. That's real success!

6. Make Money Work for You—Achieve Freedom

Your life is full of tasks, responsibilities, and problems that take up your time and energy. When you don't have money, you have to do everything yourself, stress about every little thing, and struggle through unnecessary hardships. But when you earn well and manage your money wisely, you can automate many aspects of your life and focus on what truly matters.

1. Money Saves Your Time & Energy

When you have money, you don't have to waste time on things that can be done better and faster with the right resources.

- Hiring Help – Instead of spending hours cleaning, cooking, or handling small tasks, you can hire people to do it and use your time for more productive things.

- Using Technology – You can automate bill payments, investments, savings, and even learning through online courses. No need to manually track every expense or stress about missing payments.

- Better Healthcare – With money, you can afford regular checkups, good nutrition, and fitness programs so you don't have to spend years fixing health issues that could've been prevented.

2. Money Helps You Make Smarter Decisions

When you don't have money, you're forced to take decisions based on urgency rather than what's right for you. With financial stability, you get freedom of choice.

- Choosing the Right Work – You don't have to take jobs or projects just because you need money. You can focus on what aligns with your skills and values.

- Investing in Growth – Instead of struggling for every rupee, you can invest in learning, business, or assets that grow over time.

- Buying Quality, Not Cheap – When you have money, you don't go for the cheapest option that breaks down fast. You invest in good quality that lasts, saving you time and effort in the long run.

3. Money Reduces Stress & Increases Focus

A big reason people can't focus on personal growth, relationships, or spirituality is because they're constantly worrying about money. When your financial system is in place, you can focus on higher things.

- No Panic Mode – When emergencies come, you don't have to run around borrowing money. You have savings and backups in place.

- Better Mental Peace – You can take time to relax, meditate, and think clearly instead of living in survival mode every day.

- Freedom to Enjoy Life – Travel, recreation, and spending time with family becomes easier when money is not a constant worry.

Life Lessons

- Money is not just for spending—it's for making life easier and smarter. Use it wisely.

- Don't trade all your time for money. Earn smart, so you have time for yourself and your loved ones.

- Invest in systems that reduce your stress. Automate finances, outsource tasks, and focus on things that matter.

- Financial freedom = Time freedom. When you handle money well, you get back control over your life.

So, make money, manage it well, and use it to automate life. That's how you create a life where you grow, stay stress-free, and enjoy every moment.

7. Money Helps You Live Your True Self

You would have seen many people fake their way through life just because they don't have money. They do jobs they hate, stay in relationships out of dependency, compromise their values for survival, and pretend to be someone they're not just to fit in. But when you have money, you have the freedom to be yourself, make honest choices, and live life on your own terms.

1. Money Gives You the Freedom to Be Real

When you're struggling financially, you're often forced to say yes when you want to say no or act differently just to please others.

But when you have financial stability, you don't have to fake anything.

- Work on Your Own Terms – You can choose a job, business, or profession that aligns with your values instead of doing something just for survival.

- Speak the Truth Without Fear – Many people stay silent about their real opinions because they fear losing financial support. When you have money, you can be honest without worrying about consequences.

- Make Life Decisions Based on What's Right, Not What's Necessary – You don't have to stay in toxic environments, bad jobs, or unhealthy relationships just because you need financial security.

2. Money Helps You Stay True to Your Values

People often compromise on integrity when they are financially desperate. But when you have money, you don't have to sell your soul for survival.

- You Don't Have to Cheat, Beg, or Borrow Unnecessarily – When you have enough, you can live with dignity and not depend on others.

- You Can Give Without Expecting Anything in Return – True generosity comes when you're not struggling yourself. You can help family, friends, and society in a way that feels right, not out of obligation.

- You Can Choose Growth Over Shortcuts – When you're financially stable, you don't have to take unethical shortcuts. You can build success step by step, staying honest and consistent.

3. Money Lets You Express Yourself Fully

When financial stress is out of the way, you can focus on what truly matters—your passions, purpose, and self-expression.

- Pursue Your Dreams – Whether it's art, music, travel, or social work, you can follow what you love without financial worries stopping you.

- Build Confidence – Financial security gives you the courage to make bold decisions, take risks, and believe in yourself.

- Stay Calm & Grounded – When money stress is removed, your mind is clearer, and you can make decisions based on wisdom, not desperation.

Life Lessons About Money & Authenticity

- Money is not about luxury; it's about freedom. The more financially stable you are, the more authentic you can be.

- When you don't have money, the world controls you. When you have money, you control your own life.

- Don't chase money for show—earn it to live with truth and dignity.

- The goal is not just to make money, but to make money in a way that lets you be yourself.

So, friend, earn smart, stay true, and use money to live your most authentic life. That's the real success!

8. Money Shapes Your Values, Not Just Your Lifestyle

Money isn't just about buying things; it shapes you, builds your character, and helps you grow into a better version of yourself. When you earn and manage money the right way, it naturally develops key values like courage, clarity, consistency, capacity, consciousness, and caring.

1. Money Builds Courage

When you're financially stable, you stop living in fear. Fear of the future, fear of losing a job, fear of what others think—these start fading when you have money backing you up.

- You take bold career decisions – You don't have to settle for just any job. You can take risks, start a business, or invest in your dreams.

- You stand up for yourself – Financial independence means you don't have to tolerate toxic people or situations just for survival.

- You embrace challenges – When you know you have a safety net, you dare to try new things, explore opportunities, and grow.

2. Money Brings Clarity

Money gives you the mental space to think clearly instead of always worrying about survival.

- You can plan your future – When you're not stuck in a paycheck-to-paycheck cycle, you can set real goals for your life.

- You make better choices – No desperate decisions. You pick what truly aligns with your purpose.

- You understand your priorities – You stop chasing everything and focus only on what matters—health, relationships, growth, and impact.

3. Money Develops Consistency

Success isn't about luck—it's about doing the right things consistently. Money teaches you this because it rewards those who stay disciplined.

- You build habits of earning, saving, and investing – Just like fitness, money needs daily discipline.

- You commit to your work – Whether in a job or business, financial success comes when you show up and deliver every day.

- You stay focused on long-term success – No quick money traps, no distractions. Just steady growth.

4. Money Expands Your Capacity

The more you grow financially, the more you expand your skills, knowledge, and ability to handle bigger responsibilities.

- You learn new things – Better opportunities come when you develop high-value skills.

- You manage bigger challenges – As your income grows, you become capable of handling more responsibility—whether in career, business, or life.

- You evolve as a person – Financial growth pushes you to think bigger, act smarter, and become a better version of yourself.

5. Money Increases Consciousness

When you're not drowning in financial stress, you start thinking beyond just survival.

- You become self-aware – You have the time and space to reflect on your values, purpose, and direction in life.

- You start making mindful choices – What you eat, how you spend your time, where you invest—it all becomes more conscious.

- You focus on your inner growth – Meditation, learning, and self-improvement become part of your routine when money worries aren't consuming you.

6. Money Enables Caring

True giving happens when you have enough for yourself first. Money allows you to care for your family, friends, and even society.

- You support your loved ones – Whether it's parents, siblings, or friends in need, financial strength lets you help without hesitation.

- You contribute to society – Donate, mentor, or fund causes you believe in—it all becomes possible with money.

- You become a source of strength – People around you feel safe knowing you can be relied on.

Life Lessons About Money & Values

- Money is a teacher—it forces you to be disciplined, courageous, and responsible.

- The more you grow financially, the more you grow as a person.

- Don't just earn for survival; earn for freedom, growth, and contribution.

- Your values shape your money, and your money shapes your values.

So, you make money the right way, and let it build you into a person of true strength, clarity, and purpose. That's how you win!

Money is a powerful tool that fuels freedom, growth, and opportunities—but true success goes beyond financial wealth. When you master your relationship with money and align it with your values, you unlock a deeper level of success—one where growth becomes effortless and unstoppable. Now, let's step into that ultimate state—where success flows naturally, without struggle.

9. Summary of the Chapter

Money Comes from People

Money doesn't just appear—it flows through people. Your salary, business income, or investments all come from others.

Key Lesson:

- Stop chasing money—focus on helping people and solving their problems. The more value you provide, the more money you attract.

- Your network is your net worth—surround yourself with the right people.

- Money follows trust, relationships, and service—not just effort.

Shift your mindset from "How do I make more money?" to "How can I serve more people?"

Money Solves Problems That Lack of It Creates

Most life problems—stress, broken relationships, poor health, missed opportunities—are linked to a lack of money.

Why money matters:

- Financial stress affects your health, relationships, and peace of mind.

- Without money, even maintaining what you have (home, car, lifestyle) becomes a struggle.

- Your career is your strongest money source—focus on skills, service, and ethical earning.

Earning money isn't greed—it's about avoiding problems and living with peace and dignity.

Career and Money Go Hand in Hand

Your career is the engine that drives your income. The more you grow in your profession, the more you earn.

Money = Value Creation:

- Money is a byproduct of solving problems—focus on creating impact.

- Career growth = Financial growth—stagnation in one leads to stagnation in the other.

- Money gives freedom—to travel, help family, and live on your terms.

Take your career seriously, and money will follow. Ignore it, and financial struggles begin.

The Formula for Making and Growing Money

Earning money isn't luck—it's a process.

3-Step Formula:

1. Develop Your Expertise – Be so skilled that people see your value.

2. Communicate Your Expertise – Showcase your skills at work or in business.

3. Monetize It – Confidently charge for your value—negotiate, price well, and build trust.

Key Lessons:

- Money is an exchange of value, not just time.

- Visibility creates wealth—if people don't know you, they won't pay you.

- Trust attracts money—build strong relationships and deliver value.

Master a skill, make it known, and confidently charge for it. That's how real wealth is built.

Money: The Hidden Fuel for Growth

Money is a tool—it should support every area of life, not just accumulate.

Use money for:

- Health – Fitness, nutrition, and medical care.

- Wealth – Smart investments for long-term security.

- Relationships – Supporting loved ones, spending quality time.

- Career – Continuous learning and skill-building.

- Recreation – Travel, hobbies, and rest.

- Spirituality – Inner peace, meditation, and personal growth.

- Contribution – Giving back to society and helping others.

Earn with balance—don't let money ruin your health, family, or values.

Make Money Work for You—Achieve Freedom

Money isn't just for spending—it's for saving time, reducing stress, and creating freedom.

How money frees you:

- Automate and delegate – Hire help, use tech, and free up time for higher-value work.

- Make better decisions – Financial stability lets you choose opportunities instead of chasing survival.

- Enjoy life fully – No stress about bills, emergencies, or basic needs.

Handle money well, and it will handle your life well.

Money Helps You Live Your True Self

Lack of money forces people to fake, compromise, and settle. Financial stability gives you the power to be authentic.

With money, you can:

- Choose work you love – No need to take jobs just for survival.

- Speak your truth – No fear of losing financial security.

- Make decisions based on values, not desperation.

Earn wisely, and live with dignity, honesty, and freedom.

Money Shapes Your Values, Not Just Your Lifestyle

Money is more than a tool—it builds character. The way you earn, spend, and manage money shapes your mindset and values.

How money impacts personal growth:

Courage – Financial security removes fear, letting you take bold steps.

Clarity – Less financial stress = better decision-making.

Consistency – Good financial habits create long-term success.

Capacity – Learning to earn and manage money expands your potential.

Consciousness – Wealth shifts focus from survival to higher thinking.

Caring – Financial freedom enables you to give generously.

Money, when earned and used right, makes you a stronger, wiser, and more compassionate person.

Money is a Tool—Use It Wisely

- Don't chase money—chase value creation.

- Manage money well—it should serve you, not control you.

- Use wealth to grow, give, and live a life of purpose.

Master money, and you master your life.

CHAPTER 7

UNSTOPPABLE

1. Oneness: The Key to Being Unstoppable

Let me share something truly mind-blowing with you—this will change how you see life forever!

You know how we always feel like we're separate from things? Like, "This is mine, that's yours, this is me, that's the world"? That's where all our struggles start! The moment you see that everything belongs to you, that nothing is truly separate, boom—conflict disappears! Life starts flowing.

Now, here's the crazy part—your life isn't just randomly happening. It's actually being designed by universal intelligence! The ideas you get, the insights, the "aha" moments—they aren't just yours. They are flowing through you from a higher source. You're like a channel for something much bigger.

And when you're truly in the present—like fully aware, right here, right now—you're one with life itself. No resistance, no overthinking, just pure presence. That's where real authenticity begins. It's not about forcing yourself to be someone; it's about going beyond your thoughts and actions and just witnessing.

When you do that, you realize—there's nothing you need to do to "be." You already are!

Now, let me blow your mind further. When I say generally "you," Its your body and your mind. Those are just tools. The real "you" is universal consciousness! Your mind? It's just a thought machine, creating emotions, stories, ideas. Your body? It's just the action-taker, sensing, moving. But YOU are beyond both. Both are yours.

And guess what happens when you elevate yourself to that level of awareness? You tap into something pure existence, pure knowledge, pure bliss! Your being transcends all limits. Your wisdom expands infinitely. And your ability to act with purpose skyrockets. You become truly unstoppable!

Most people think their intellect is what makes decisions, compares options, and analyzes things. But the deeper truth? There's something even beyond intellect—a pure consciousness that orchestrates everything. It's constantly shaping your body, mind, and environment. When you sync with that, you stop struggling, and life just flows.

So, here's the takeaway—your life, your path, your experiences? They're already designed. When you stop resisting and start recognizing that everything happening inside and around you is part of this universal intelligence, magic happens.

Once you see this, you'll never look at life the same way again. You'll move through life with clarity, confidence, and total freedom. And that, my friend, is what unstoppable success truly looks like!

2. Why Your Success is Unstoppable

Hello Friend, let me tell you something truly exciting—this success we're talking about? It's unstoppable! And here's why...

Most people think success is about hard work, luck, or strategies. But let me reveal the real secret—true success isn't something you chase. It's something you align with. And once you do, nothing can stop it.

See, when you realize that nothing is separate from you, conflict disappears. The struggle, the doubts, the fears—all gone! Why? Because you're no longer fighting against life. You're flowing with it. And when you flow with life, life works for you.

Now, here's where it gets even better. Your life? It's not random. It's already designed by universal intelligence! The thoughts you get, the knowledge you gain, even the challenges you face—they're all part of this grand design. And the best part? This intelligence is working through you at every moment. You're not alone in this journey.

Think about it—when you're fully present, when you stop overthinking and just be, you tap into something much bigger. You're no longer a slave to your mind and body. Instead, you witness them, and in that awareness, you become truly authentic.

And here's the real magic—when you rise above your limited self and connect with universal consciousness, your power explodes! Your being becomes infinite, your knowledge deepens, and your ability to act with clarity becomes effortless. This is the state of pure existence, pure awareness, and pure bliss!

This is why your success is unstoppable—because it's not about struggling to "make things happen." It's about recognizing that things are already happening through you, as part of a higher plan. And when you align with that, you don't just grow—you thrive effortlessly.

So, forget chasing success. Instead, step into this awareness, trust the intelligence working through you, and watch how life opens doors you never even knew existed.

Unstoppable success isn't something you create—it's something you allow. And once you allow it, there's no force in the world that can stop it!

Exciting, right? This changes everything!

"You Are Unstoppable: Align with the Ultimate Power!"

Friend, let me tell you something that will blow your mind—you are unstoppable! Not because of luck, not because of hard work alone, but because you are connected to something much bigger—a collective intelligence that guides everything!

Think about it—have you ever had a gut feeling that turned out to be right? Or an idea that just "came to you" out of nowhere? That's not random! That's your intellect receiving pre-designed signals—guidance from universal intelligence. When you trust those signals, success doesn't just happen—it becomes inevitable!

And you know what? The ancient wisdom ,the ultimate universal principle "Tat Tvam Asi"—which means *You are That*—tells us exactly this. You are not separate from the universe. The intelligence that moves the planets, grows the trees, and beats your heart—it's the same intelligence that drives your success! When you align with it, you don't just move—you flow.

Now, here's the secret sauce: your free will is the key to unlocking this power. When you actively start self awareness, the entire universe starts working in your favor. Life stops being a battle, and everything begins to align perfectly for you. That's why some people seem to have effortless success—they're not fighting against life; they're moving with it.

And here's where it gets really powerful—when you are in touch with the 12 elements of intentional habit, you automatically align with your true self. You feel centered, powerful, and completely clear in your actions. No doubts. No hesitation. Just pure confidence and flow.

This is why authenticity is your superpower. The more real you are, the less resistance you face. You don't have to force things. The right people, the right opportunities, and the right results come naturally to you because you are working with life, not against it.

And here's the ultimate hack for unstoppable success—when you work, work as if everything depends on you. Give it your all, push beyond limits, and show up 100%. But when you think, think as if everything depends on the universal intelligence. Trust the signals, let go of fear, and allow the higher power to guide you. This balance between effort and surrender creates an unstoppable force within you.

So, my friend, the truth is simple—you are already designed for success. When you trust the signals, align with the universal flow, and act with full power, there is NOTHING that can stop you!

This is the path to limitless success. And the best part? You already have everything you need inside you!

Now, tell me—are you ready to step into your unstoppable self?

3. The Blueprint for Unstoppable Success

Friend, let me tell you something powerful — success isn't something you chase; it's something you become. And once you align yourself with this, nothing can stop you!

The secret? Live with purpose, serve with passion, and grow effortlessly. Let's break it down in the simplest way:

1. Prosperity Through Service

Forget just making money—real prosperity is about impact. The more you serve, the more abundance flows to you.

- True fulfillment comes from knowing your work is changing lives.

- Give without expectation, and life will reward you beyond measure.

- Align your work with a purpose, and success becomes automatic.

Key insight: Success follows those who create value for others. Serve first, and prosperity will chase you!

2. The Power of Creativity, Productivity & Profitability

These three are the fuel for your unstoppable growth:

- Creativity brings fresh ideas and solutions.

- Productivity ensures those ideas turn into reality.

- Profitability sustains your journey—because when you create real value, abundance follows.

Key insight: Think differently, act consistently, and let success multiply effortlessly.

3. Leadership Through Service

Want to be a leader? Don't try to control—serve.

- Lead by example: Show up with courage, clarity, and consistency.

- Empower others: A true leader lifts people up, not commands from above.

- Earn trust, not demand respect: Influence happens naturally when people see your authenticity.

Key insight: The more people you help succeed, the bigger your success becomes!

4. The Formula for Unstoppable Success

It's simple: Be, Don't Chase. Success isn't about adding more tasks—it's about aligning with your true self.

- Live with courage, clarity, and consistency.

- Tap into your limitless potential by trusting your intuition.

- Stop struggling—flow with universal intelligence, and life will guide you.

Key insight: When you step into your authentic self, success becomes effortless!

5. The Daily Practice for Sustained Growth

Here's the magic formula: Just 12 minutes a day can transform your life!

- Reflect on the 12 elements—body, breath, mind, intellect, memory, ego, self,etc...

- Embody the 6 C's: Courage, Clarity, Consistency, Capacity, Consciousness, and Caring.

- Stay present & celebrate progress. Growth is a journey, not a race!

Key insight: Small, consistent actions lead to unstoppable success!

6. The Ultimate Freedom: Happiness, Growth & Prosperity

What's the final goal? A life of:

- Happiness – Aligning with your true self.

- Freedom – Letting go of unnecessary burdens.

- Prosperity – The natural result of serving and growing.

Key insight: Live authentically, grow consistently, and success will be your default state.

This Is Just the Beginning!

Everything you need for success is already within you. The universe is guiding you. Now, take the first step:

- Dedicate your 12 minutes.

- Embrace the 6 C's.

- Step into the life you were meant to live!

This isn't just a strategy—it's a way of life. And when you commit to it, your success becomes unstoppable.

Now, tell me—are you ready to claim the life that's already meant for you?

4. The Effortless Path to Growth

Friend, let's talk about something that will change the way you see life forever. Why do we struggle? Why do we feel stuck? The answer is simple: we mistakenly believe we are just our body and mind. But the truth is, you are way beyond that. Once you get this, success, peace, and freedom become effortless. Let me explain.

1. You Are Not Just Your Body and Mind

Most of our suffering comes from identifying too much with our body and mind. We think, "This is happening to me because of me." But what if I told you everything is already designed and communicated through you?

- The universal intelligence is working through your mind to create thoughts.

- Your body acts according to that same intelligence.

- Even your free will is part of this grand design.

Life is not happening to you. Life is happening through you!

2. Everything is One—Separation Creates Conflict

Ever noticed how stress, doubt, and fear only come when we feel separate from everything else? The moment you think, "This is mine, that is yours," conflicts begin. But everything is connected—living and non-living, seen and unseen.

- Your thoughts create another world inside your head, different from reality.

- But if you just observe without thinking, you'll realize life is simple, effortless, and already perfect.

- You don't have to fix anything—just be in the moment and witness how life unfolds.

The mind complicates, but reality is simple. Drop the extra thoughts, and life becomes easy.

3. Live in the Present—It's the Gift of Life

You ever feel like life is overwhelming? That's because you're either stuck in the past or worrying about the future. The present moment is all you ever truly have.

- Without thoughts, just observe your body, your mind, and your environment.

- That's when you feel completely alive—because you are not lost in illusions.

- Your intellect is always creating and changing things as per universal design.

You don't have to control life—just experience it fully, right now.

4. Life is Happening Effortlessly—Stop Trying So Hard

We are taught that hard work leads to success. But what if I told you that life is already happening as per the universal design? The supreme consciousness is constantly:

- Creating what's needed.

- Sustaining what serves its purpose.

- Destroying what's no longer needed.

So, stop forcing things. Let go of struggle. Align with this intelligence, and life flows naturally.

When you stop pushing against life, life starts working for you.

5. The Truth is Already in You—No Need to Search

You don't need a method, a practice, or a secret formula to find your true self. It's already there.

- You don't have to "achieve" self-realization. You are already that.

- The only thing needed is awareness—simply knowing this truth.

- Whether you speak in words or stay silent, you are still connected to the universal intelligence.

Just be. That's enough.

6. Success, Peace, and Freedom are Natural Outcomes

When you understand that:

- You are beyond body and mind.

- Life is already designed to unfold effortlessly

- You don't need to chase happiness—it's already in you

...then what's left to struggle with? Success comes naturally. Happiness is automatic. Freedom is your reality.

You are already complete. Life is already taking care of itself. Just align, observe, and flow.

Let Go & Let Life Happen!

Look, my friend, this is not some deep philosophy. It's the simplest truth ever: Life is effortless when you stop resisting it.

- Stop overthinking. Just experience.

- Stop trying so hard. Just be.

- Stop chasing success. Align with reality, and success follows.

You don't have to struggle anymore. Just step into the present, let go of unnecessary thoughts, and watch how unstoppable you become.

Now tell me—are you ready to let go and truly live?

5. How to Succeed Without Struggle

Friend, let's clear up a big misconception that's keeping most people stuck. People think they are in full control of everything happening to them. But when you believe that, you suffer—

because you take every success, failure, or struggle personally. The truth is way bigger and way simpler.

Let me show you how to break free and automate your growth effortlessly.

1. You Are Not the Doer—Life is Happening Through You

We think, "I did this," or "This happened because of me." But is that really true?

- Every thought, action, and even your body is a product of universal intelligence working through you.

- Not even a tiny atom moves without the universal will.

- Your intellect receives signals, passes instructions, and aligns your actions.

Life is not something you manually control—it flows through you!

So instead of overthinking, align with reality and flow with life. That's where real power is.

2. Authenticity is the Key to Effortless Success

Do you know what makes you unstoppable? Being authentic.

When you are true to yourself, you naturally develop:

- Courage to face life boldly.

- Clarity in decisions.

- Consistency in actions.

- Greater Capacity to handle challenges.

- Higher Consciousness to see life beyond the surface.

- A natural desire to help and contribute to others.

Authenticity removes resistance. It aligns you with success, so growth happens automatically.

No need for struggle—just be real.

3. Stop Wasting Energy on Useless Stuff

Look around—why do people feel drained and unfulfilled?

- They chase happiness outside—through social media, drinking, smoking, or trends.

- They talk a lot but don't take meaningful action.

- They waste time in unproductive thoughts instead of experiencing real life.

The moment you stop engaging in distractions, your energy gets redirected toward unstoppable success.

Do less—be more. Focus on what truly matters.

4. The Hardest Thing is Looking Within

Let me ask you—how easy is it to judge others? Super easy, right?

But the toughest challenge is looking at yourself and asking:

"Who am I? What am I doing? What is real?"

Most people fear self-reflection—they'd rather stay distracted. But the truth is:

- Happiness is within you—not outside.

- Success is about alignment, not effort.

- Reality flows when you stop resisting it.

The moment you turn inward, you unlock the easiest path to success. No more struggle—just effortless progress.

5. When You Live in Reality, Life Becomes Effortless

When you let go of false beliefs, external distractions, and unnecessary resistance, life stops feeling like a fight.

- Struggles fade.

- Things align easily.

- Growth becomes natural.

You don't chase success anymore—it starts coming to you.

Unstoppable success is not about doing more—it's about doing the right things effortlessly.

Automate Your Growth, Free Yourself!

Friend, the real secret is this: stop complicating life.

- You are not just a body or mind—you are beyond that.

- Stop wasting energy on unproductive thoughts and distractions.

- Be authentic, and everything falls into place naturally.

Success, happiness, and fulfillment are already within you—just align, observe, and let life flow. That's the secret to being unstoppable!

So tell me, are you ready to stop struggling and start flowing with life?

6. Flow Over Force: The Secret to Unstoppable Success

Hello friend, let's get real—why do most people feel stuck? Why does life feel like a constant struggle? It's not because of external problems, but because we are cluttered inside.

Our subconscious mind is filled with old patterns, beliefs, and unnecessary resistance. If you want to become an authentic, unstoppable personality, you have to release this resistance and flow with life.

Let's break it down.

1. Thinking Limits You—Experiencing Sets You Free

Most people think too much—but what does thinking really do?

- It just manipulates data and justifies what you already believe.

- Discovery doesn't happen through logic—it happens through knowing and being.

- The truth is always present and real—whether you accept it or not.

If you keep analyzing life, you'll stay trapped in thought. If you experience life, you'll live in truth.

2. Thoughts Are the Real Culprit

Want a better life? Think less.

- Thoughts take you to the past and future, keeping you away from the now.

- Thoughts create an imaginary world filled with pleasure, pain, doubts, and fears.

- The lesser the thoughts, the better the life.

Drop unnecessary thoughts, and you'll see reality clearly.

3. Intuition is Your Original Response

Ever noticed when someone asks you a question, your first instinctive answer is often the best?

- That's your real intelligence.

- But then thoughts step in and pull you in different directions.

Trust your first intuitive response—it's often the most authentic.

4. You See Reality Only When Thoughts Don't Interfere

When you look at a person or a situation without thoughts, you see the truth.

- The moment thoughts enter, you see only what your mind wants to see.

- That's why people judge, assume, and create false perceptions.

Stop filtering reality—just experience it as it is.

5. A 12-Minute Habit to Transform Your Life

The fastest way to experience reality effortlessly?

A 12-minute daily practice that helps you:

- Remove mental clutter.

- Align with your natural flow.

- Become more authentic.

When you start living in reality, success becomes automatic. No resistance, no struggle—just natural growth.

6. Authenticity = Accepting Reality

Being authentic is not about being perfect. It's about dealing with life as it is.

- Reality exists without thoughts.

- You are not in control of everything—life happens through universal intelligence.

- Free will is part of destiny—it happens with your conscious effort, while fate unfolds around you.

Stop fighting reality. Accept it, flow with it, and you'll experience unstoppable success.

7. Don't Worry About Tomorrow—Live Now

Most people stress about what will happen tomorrow. But here's the truth:

- What's happening now is the only reality.

- Perception is our only real knowledge.

- Thinking about the future only creates unnecessary worry.

Focus on NOW—because NOW is the only thing that truly exists.

8. Confidence Comes from Action, Not Thoughts

Want real confidence? It's not about motivational quotes—it's about your approach to life.

- Self-Efficacy → "Yes, I can do it."

- Self-Responsibility → "Yes, I will take ownership."

- Self-Direction → "Yes, I have clear goals."

Confidence is the result of doing, not thinking.

9. The Final Truth: There's Nothing to Learn for Happiness

Most people keep searching for happiness, thinking they are missing something. But the secret is:

- You already have everything you need to be happy.

- Your doubts are the only thing stopping you.

- Observe your thoughts, align with your destiny, and act with the least resistance.

Automate your growth—flow with life, and happiness will naturally follow.

Effortless Growth is the Goal

Friend, don't complicate life. Success and happiness are already within you.

- Drop unnecessary thoughts.

- Trust your intuition.

- Flow with reality, not against it.

- Live in the NOW.

- Stop searching—just BE.

This is how you become unstoppable—without struggle!

So tell me, are you ready to stop thinking and start experiencing life?

7. Summary of the Chapter

1. Oneness: The Key to Being Unstoppable

Most struggles in life come from feeling separate—from people, success, and even the universe. The moment you realize that everything is connected, life starts flowing effortlessly.

Key Insights:

- You are not just your body or mind—you are universal consciousness.

- Life is already designed—your thoughts, ideas, and experiences are guided by higher intelligence.

- Struggle happens when you resist—but when you sync with this intelligence, you step into limitless power and wisdom.

When you stop resisting and start witnessing, you become truly unstoppable.

2. Why Your Success is Unstoppable

Success isn't about chasing—it's about aligning. The universe is already working through you to create success.

Why success flows naturally:

- You are connected to universal intelligence—the same force that moves planets and grows trees.

- Your intuition receives pre-designed signals—trust them, and success becomes inevitable.

- You are not fighting against life anymore—you are moving with it.

When you align with this flow, you don't just grow—you thrive effortlessly.

3. The Blueprint for Unstoppable Success

Success follows a simple, natural flow—not struggle or force.

6 Pillars of Unstoppable Success:

1. Prosperity Through Service – The more people you serve, the more abundance flows to you.

2. Creativity, Productivity & Profitability – Think differently, act consistently, and let success multiply.

3. Leadership Through Service – True leaders lift others up, not command from above.

4. The Formula for Success – Be authentic—don't chase. Align with your purpose, and success follows.

5. The Daily Practice – A 12-minute habit can transform your life.

6. The Ultimate Freedom – Happiness, growth, and prosperity happen when you live in alignment.

Stop chasing success. Align with it, and it will chase you.

4. The Effortless Path to Growth

Why do we struggle? Because we think we are in control. The truth? Life is already designed.

How to grow effortlessly:

- You are not your thoughts—observe them, don't get trapped in them.

- Life is simple—separation creates conflict—when you stop overthinking, peace follows.

- Success happens when you stop forcing it—growth unfolds naturally when you align with reality.

Let go of struggle. Just witness, and life will take care of the rest.

5. How to Succeed Without Struggle

Most people believe they are in full control of their success. This mindset leads to stress, doubt, and suffering. The truth? Life happens through you, not because of you.

How to automate your success:

- You are not the doer—life is flowing through universal intelligence.

- Authenticity removes resistance—when you are real, success happens effortlessly.

- Stop wasting energy on useless distractions—focus on what truly matters.

Success isn't about effort—it's about alignment.

6. Flow Over Force: The Secret to Unstoppable Success

Most people live in mental clutter—old patterns, limiting beliefs, and unnecessary resistance. To be truly unstoppable, release that resistance and flow with life.

How to master the flow:

- Thinking limits you—experiencing sets you free.

- Your intuition is your original intelligence—trust it.

- Thoughts distort reality—see life without filters.

- Success, peace, and happiness are already within you.

Drop unnecessary thoughts, align with life, and success will follow naturally.

You Are Already Unstoppable

- Stop chasing, start aligning.

- Let go of struggle—flow with life.

- Success is not something you achieve—it's something you allow.

The universe is guiding you. Trust, align, and step into your unstoppable self!

CONCLUSION

ello friend,

You've come a long way through this journey, and now we stand at the final chapter—but let me tell you, this is just the beginning of something incredible.

We started with one simple truth: Growth is inevitable, but transformation is a choice. You can either struggle through life, constantly trying to figure things out, or you can automate your growth, making success, happiness, and freedom a natural part of your existence.

Now, let's connect the dots one last time—so you see how everything comes together and how this book is about to make a real difference in your life.

The Path to Automating Your Growth

1. Automate – Life operates on a pre-designed flow, just like the universe. You don't need to fight for success—you need to align with the right process. The secret is to stop overthinking and take effortless, consistent action toward the life you want.

2. Habit – Growth isn't about grand efforts; it's about small, repeated actions. The 12-minute daily habit I've shared is your

key to rewiring your mind and making growth an automatic process.

3. Authentic – You don't need to become someone else to be successful. The real power lies in being yourself—without masks, without fear. When you align with your true self, life stops being a struggle.

4. Values – Strength comes from your core values—Courage, Clarity, Consistency, Capacity, Consciousness, and Caring. These aren't just words; they are the foundation that makes you unshakable in any situation.

5. Growth – If you don't grow intentionally, life will push you in directions you don't want. Holistic growth means balancing health, wealth, relationships, career, contribution, recreation, and spirituality—so that no part of your life is left behind.

6. Money – Money isn't just about numbers; it's a tool for freedom. When you understand how to earn, manage, and use money wisely, you gain the power to design your life on your terms.

7. Unstoppable – The ultimate goal? To live in flow, not in force. Once you drop resistance and start trusting the universal

intelligence working through you, success stops being something you "chase"—it becomes something you allow.

How This Book Will Make a Difference in Your Life

- No More Overthinking – You'll finally break free from the doubts and fears that hold you back.

- Consistency Without Struggle – Growth won't feel like a battle anymore—it will happen naturally.

- True Transformation – You won't just "achieve" success; you will become a person for whom success is automatic.

- Freedom in Every Sense – Financial, emotional, and spiritual freedom—because when you grow in the right way, everything aligns.

- Living with Purpose & Impact – You'll wake up each day with clarity, knowing exactly where your life is going.

Your Next Steps: Action Points for Readers

1. Start Your 12-Minute Daily Habit – No excuses. This is the foundation of automating your growth.

2. Live by Your Values – Every day, ask yourself: Am I acting with courage, clarity, and consistency, capacity,

consciousness and caring? If the answer is YES, you're on the right path.

3. Make Growth Holistic – Don't just focus on one area of life—balance health, wealth, relationships, career, and beyond.

4. Change Your Relationship with Money – See money as a tool for growth and start managing it wisely to create freedom.

5. Trust the Flow – Stop forcing things. Align with who you are meant to be, and success will start coming effortlessly.

Final Words: Wishing You a Life of Freedom, Growth & Unstoppable Success

My friend, this knowledge isn't just theory—it's the ultimate life strategy that can change everything for you. But remember, knowing is not enough—you have to apply it.

So, here's my final message to you:

- Live with courage.

- Act with clarity.

- Stay consistent.

- Expand your capacity.

- Be fully conscious.

- Care deeply and contribute.

And above all—trust the process.

Your growth is now automated, your success is unstoppable, and your life is yours to design.

I wish you a life of abundance, joy, and freedom.

Now go out there and make it happen!

With all my heart,

Pradeepkumar K Padmanabhan

SUMMARY OF THE BOOK

Automate Your Growth is a transformative guide designed to help you unlock unstoppable success by making personal growth automatic, effortless, and natural. Through a structured, repeatable 12-minute daily habit, this book helps you eliminate resistance, cultivate authenticity, and align your life with your true potential.

Key Insights from the Book:

Automate Growth – Learn to work with life instead of against it. Just like the universe follows a natural rhythm, your success should flow effortlessly.

The 12-Minute Habit – A simple yet powerful daily practice that rewires your mind, strengthens your values, and ensures consistent, sustainable growth without overwhelming effort.

Authenticity is the Key – True success isn't about becoming someone else—it's about becoming more of who you truly are by removing resistance and aligning with your natural strengths.

The Power of Values – Six core values—Courage, Clarity, Consistency, Capacity, Consciousness, and Caring—form the foundation of unshakable success.

Holistic Growth – Personal and professional success go hand in hand. This book helps you expand in all seven areas of life—health, wealth, relationships, career, recreation, contribution, and spirituality.

Money as a Tool for Freedom – Learn how to use money wisely—not just to accumulate wealth, but to fuel your growth, purpose, and freedom.

Becoming Unstoppable – By aligning your intellect, values, and actions, you enter a state of flow where success no longer feels like a struggle—it happens naturally.

DISCLAIMER

The information in ***Automate Your Growth*** is provided for educational and informational purposes only. While this book is based on my 30+ years of experience in coaching, mentoring, and business, it does not constitute professional financial, psychological, or legal advice. Every individual's circumstances are unique, and readers are encouraged to use their judgment, seek professional guidance, and adapt the strategies to their personal situations.

The methods and insights shared in this book are designed to help you cultivate sustainable growth, but results may vary based on individual effort, consistency, and external factors. This book does not promise guaranteed success, financial gain, or specific outcomes.

The author and publisher disclaim any liability for any direct, indirect, or consequential loss or damage arising from the use of this book or its contents.

By reading ***Automate Your Growth,*** you acknowledge that personal growth is a journey requiring continuous effort, and you take full responsibility for applying the principles discussed.

About The Author

Pradeepkumar K Padmanabhan |
Ex-Army Officer | Engineer | Techpreneur | Engineers' Growth Coach|

Pradeepkumar K Padmanabhan (Capt Pradeepkumar KP, Retd.) is an Ex-Army Officer and is an accomplished Engineer, Techpreneur, and Engineers' Growth Coach with over 30 years of diverse industry experience. His journey spans from serving as a Technical Officer in the Indian Army to leading multiple entrepreneurial ventures, and now, mentoring engineers to achieve prosperity, freedom, and purpose.

A Career of Impact and Innovation

Pradeepkumar's professional journey began in private companies, a public sector organization, and the Indian Army. Later, he transitioned into entrepreneurship, founding and leading two private limited companies and multiple proprietary firms.

Now, his true calling is empowering engineers—helping them build purpose-driven careers, achieve financial success, and create a balanced life.

The TRUE Mission – Transforming Engineers to Their Best

Throughout his career, Pradeepkumar observed that many engineers struggle with job dissatisfaction, low performance, and unemployment—primarily due to mindset misalignment. He realized that success comes from aligning engineers with their profession and unlocking the potential of underutilized technical resources.

This insight led him to establish the TRUE Growth Model, creating a new breed of professionals known as Technical Resource Utilization Experts (TRUE®). His mission is to transform engineers into authentic, competitive, and responsible leaders—whether in a job or business.

Through his proven strategies, he helps engineers:

Expertize – Master technical, communication, and leadership skills

Communicate – Build influence, confidence, and credibility

Monetize – Leverage skills and knowledge to create high-income opportunities

Innovate with Integrity – Drive sustainable success while making a meaningful impact

Join the Movement – Engineer Your Success!

Pradeepkumar K Padmanabhan is on a mission to help 1,000,000 engineers break free from limitations and achieve high growth, professional fulfillment, and happy living.

His book, Automate Your Growth, reflects this philosophy—offering a structured, sustainable approach to cultivating authenticity, removing resistance, and achieving holistic success.

Through his coaching and mentorship, he empowers engineers to expertise, communicate and monetize their engineering skills and knowledge.

To know more details.

Email: pradeepdesign@gmail.com

Website: www.pradeepkumarkp.com

Unlock your true potential today!

May I Ask You For A Small Favor?

First, I want to thank you for reading this book. You could have chosen any other book, but you took mine, and I appreciate this. I hope you have at least a few actionable insights that will positively impact your daily life.

Can I ask for 30 seconds more of your time?

I'd love it if you could leave a review of the book. That will help me grow my readership by encouraging folks to take a chance on my books.

Keeping it straight - reviews are the lifeblood of any author.

It will take less than a minute of your time but will tremendously help me reach out to more people.

If you liked this book, please consider posting an honest review on your preferred retailer. And I'd love to see your review. Thanks for your support.